Dawes Gobright

The Union Sketch-Book

A reliable guide, exhibiting the history and business resources of the leading mercantile and manufacturing firms of New York.

Dawes Gobright

The Union Sketch-Book
A reliable guide, exhibiting the history and business resources of the leading mercantile and manufacturing firms of New York.

ISBN/EAN: 9783337418915

Printed in Europe, USA, Canada, Australia, Japan

Cover: Foto ©ninafisch / pixelio.de

More available books at **www.hansebooks.com**

THE
UNION SKETCH-BOOK:
A Reliable Guide,

EXHIBITING THE

HISTORY AND BUSINESS RESOURCES OF THE LEADING
MERCANTILE AND MANUFACTURING
FIRMS OF NEW YORK.

INTERSPERSED WITH MANY IMPORTANT, VALUABLE, AND
INTERESTING FACTS RELATING TO THE VARIOUS
BRANCHES OF

TRADE, MANUFACTURE, AND THE MECHANIC ARTS.

TO WHICH IS ADDED

A DIRECTORY

TO THE PRINCIPAL OBJECTS OF INTEREST IN NEW YORK, AND
OTHER ITEMS OF INTEREST,

FOR THE USE OF VISITING MERCHANTS.

WRITTEN, ARRANGED, AND COMPILED FROM AUTHENTIC SOURCES.

By GOBRIGHT AND DAWES.

NEW YORK:
RUDD & CARLETON, 130 GRAND STREET.
M DCCC LXI.

JOHNS & CROSLEY,

Sole Manufacturers of the

IMPROVED

GUTTA PERCHA CEMENT ROOFING.

The Cheapest and Most Durable Roofing in use. Is Fire and Water Proof. Can be applied to Roofs of all kinds, new or old, steep or flat. The cost is less than one-half that of Tin, and is twice as durable.

GUTTA PERCHA CEMENT,

For Preserving and Repairing Tin and other Metal Roofs, is more durable, when applied to Metals of all kinds, than any Paint known, and far cheaper.

Also, Sole Manufacturers of the

AMERICAN CEMENT GLUE,

For Cementing Wood, Leather, Glass, China, Marble, Ivory, Bone, Porcelain, &c., &c.

JOHNS & CROSLEY,

WHOLESALE WAREHOUSE,

78 William Street, corner of Liberty,

NEW YORK.

FULL DESCRIPTIVE CIRCULARS FURNISHED ON APPLICATION.

INDEX.

	PAGE
Agricultural Implements, &c., *Griffing Bros.*	112
Alcohol, Camphene, &c., *J. A. Webb & Co.*	130
Alcohol and Liquors, *Hoffman & Curtis*	145
Ales, Wines, &c., *G. E. Mendum*	134
American Gutta Percha Roofing Co., *Forbes & Willis*	55
American Porcelain Photograph Co., ————	185
American Cement Glue, *Johns & Crosley*	85
Amusements, Places of, *in New York*	117
Artificial Flowers, *R. M. Mitchill*	91
Bankers, *Duncan, Sherman & Co.*	183
Billiard Tables, *Phelan & Collender*	87
Billiard Materials, *Phelan & Collender*	87
Billiard Saloons, *in New York*	115
Burning Fluid, Alcohol, &c., *J. A. Webb*	130
Candles, Soaps, &c., *J. C. Hull's Son*	12
Camphene, Alcohol, &c., *J. A. Webb*	130
Central Park, *New York*	8
City Hospital, *New York*	174
City Railroads, *New York*	82
Cigars, Wines, &c., *Thomas G. Little*	48
Cloths, Cassimeres, &c., *Sullivan, Randolph & Budd*	109
Coal Oils, &c., *Cossens & Co.*	70
Colt's Arms Company, *Hartford, Conn.*	159
Conn. Mutual Life Insurance Co., *W. S. Dunham*	128
Cordage, Twine, &c., *Willard Harvey & Co.*	127
Cracker Bakery, *E. Treadwell's Sons*	41
Currier's Oil, *Hastings & Co.*	88
Daguerreotypes, Photographs, &c., *C. D. Fredericks & Co*	50
do. do. do. *J. Gurney & Son*	58
Distillers and Rectifiers, *Hoffman & Curtiss*	145
Distances in the City, *New York*	136
Dry Goods, &c., *C. W. & J. T. Moore & Co.*	78
Drugs and Chemicals, *Schieffelin Bros. & Co.*	16
Druggists' Articles, *Schieffelin Bros. & Co.*	16
Drugs, Medicines, &c., *A. B. Sands & Co.*	142
Envelopes, *Berlin & Jones*	103
Engraving, Electrotyping. &c., *A. H. Jocelyn*	175
Feathers, for Millinery, *R. M. Mitchill*	91
Fine Art Institutions, *New York*	115
Fire Arms, *Colt's Arms Company*	159
Fancy Goods, *Cary, Howard, Sanger & Co.*	170
Fences, N. Y. Co.'s Patent, *W. Shattuck*	178
Fire Proof Safes, *S. C. Herring & Co.*	181
Gutta Percha Roofing and Cement, *Forbes & Willis*	55
Gutta Percha Cement Roofing, *Johns & Crosley*	83
Guide to Objects of Interest, *in New York*	61
Gunpowder, *The Hazard Gunpowder Company*	156
Hackney Coach Fares, *in New York*	137
Hazard Gunpowder Company	156
History of the Manufacture of Envelopes, *Berlin & Jones*	103
Hoop Skirts, *L. A. Osborn*	139
Hotels, *in New York*	96

INDEX.

	PAGE
Japanned and Planished Tin Ware, *J. D. Locke*	27
Johns & Crosley's Advertisements	2 and 4
Kerosene and Coal Oil, *Cozzens & Co.*	79
Lead Pipe, Sheet Lead, Shot, &c., *Otis, Leroy & Co.*	169
Life Insurance, *W. S. Dunham*	123
Liquors, Domestic, *Hoffman & Curties*	145
Locks, Jones' Patent, *C. S. Herring & Co.*	131
Medicines, Drugs, &c., *A. B. Sands & Co.*	142
Military Books, *D. Van Nostrand*	188
Millinery Goods, *R. M. Mitchill*	91
New York Fence Company, *W. Shattuck*	178
New York City	7
New York City Hospital	174
New York City Parks	29
Objects of Interest, *in New York City*	61
Oils, Candles, &c., *Hastings & Co.*	88
Oils, Coal, *Cozzens & Co.*	70
Paper, Envelopes, &c., *Berlin & Jones*	108
Perfumery and Toilet Articles, *Schieffelin Bros. & Co.*	16
Piano Fortes, *Lights & Bradbury*	88
do. do. *Raven, Bacon & Co.*	152
Photographic Gallery, *J. Gurney & Son*	58
Photographs, Daguerreotypes, &c., *C. D. Fredericks & Co.*	50
Population of the United States, *Census* 1860	75
Popular Resorts, *in New York*	117
Porcelain, Photographs on	185
Principal Objects of Interest *in New York*	61
Railroad Depots, *New York*	31
Roofing Patent, *Johns & Crosley*	83
Roofing, Gutta Percha, *Forbes & Willis*	55
Roofing Paint, *Forbes & Willis*	outside cover.
Saleratus, Bi-Carb. Soda, &c., *Thos. Andrews & Co.*	22
Scientific Books, *D. Van Nostrand*	188
Sewing Machines, *Grover, Baker & Co.*	66
do. do. *Wheeler, Wilson & Co.*	93
Seeds and Agricultural Implements, *Griffing Bros.*	112
Ship Bread and Crackers, *E. Treadwell's Sons*	41
Shot, Bullets, Lead, &c., *Otis, Leroy & Co.*	169
Silver Ware, *Gale & Willis*	93
Soap, Candles, &c., *Hastings & Co.*	88
do. do. *J. C. Hull's Son*	12
Soda, Saleratus, &c., *Thos. Andrews & Co.*	22
Something about Dry Goods, *C. W. & J. T. Moore & Co.*	78
Spring Bed Bottoms, *Johns & Crosley*	85
Tesselated Pavements, *Maw & Co.*	119
Theatres, *in New York*	117
Tiles for Floors, *Maw & Co.*	119
Tin Ware, &c., *J. D. Locke & Co.*	27
Twine Seines, &c., *Willard, Hurrey & Co.*	127
Ulmer Spring Bed Bottom, *Johns & Crosley*	85
Vestings, Cloths, &c., *Sullivan, Randolph & Budd*	109
Whale Oils, *Hastings & Co.*	88
Wines, Cigars, &c., *Thos. G. Little*	48
Wood Engraving, *A. H. Jocelyn*	175
Yeast Powders, *Thos. Andrews & Co.*	22

THE UNION SKETCH-BOOK AND GUIDE TO NEW YORK.

In presenting our fifth volume to the public, we would thank them for the gratifying evidences they have given us of their appreciation of our past efforts, which, in writing the present work, have impelled us to endeavor to surpass the former ones. Our aim has been, in this volume, to embody in the most condensed form, all the most important and interesting facts relating to the origin and progress of Science, Art, Mechanics, and Manufactures, and while giving many statistics we have endeavored to connect with them many interesting items that should render the book both amusing and instructive. We have added several new features to the present work which we hope will be found valuable to all into whose hands it may fall.

NEW YORK.

> 'Tis pleasant, through the loopholes of retreat,
> To peep at such a world; to see the stir
> Of the great Babel, and not feel the crowd;
> To hear the roar she sends through all her gates,
> At a safe distance, where the dying sound
> Falls a soft murmur on the uninjured ear.
>
> COWPER.

A writer of recent date thus briefly, but forcibly, refers to this metropolis—the great point of centralization for the enterprise of the entire continent. It is "the centre from which radiates most of what constitutes the prosperity and glory of the country, and to which it is directed, as the threads which comprise the spider's web all tend to the nucleus in its middle. The commerce, the learning, the scientific knowledge concentrated here—nay, the very geographical position of New York, with its two water approaches opening into the ocean, covered with a net-work of steamships—the two magnificent rivers which encircle it; the railroads which converge in its very heart, all tend to make it the centre of civilization on the American continent. Add to which it is thought to be as healthy a spot as any in the world."

It now occupies the entire island from the Battery to the Harlem river, about fourteen miles in extent, or an area of nearly twenty-three square miles. In 1850 upward of three thousand buildings were erected. During subsequent years the ratio has been much greater, while the edifices exhibit the most lavish expenditure; all tending to prove the fact that New York does business on a large scale. One of its latest and grandest enterprises is

THE GREAT CENTRAL PARK,

the lands of which came into the possession of the city in February, 1856.

DESCRIPTION OF THE GROUND.—The tract comprises at present 840 acres, including about 142 acres belonging to the Croton Aqueduct Department; and it contains, besides streets and avenues, about 9,000 lots (25 × 100). Its cost was $5,444,369.90, of which sum $1,657,590 was assessed on adjoining property, leaving $3,786,779 to be paid by the city, the money being borrowed on five per cent. stock, payable in 1898. This is believed to have been the largest sum ever expended in the purchase of land for a public park. The park, as its name implies, lies in the geographical centre of New York Island, being about five miles from the Battery and from King's Bridge, and about three quarters of a mile from the East river and from the North river. It is about two and a half miles long, and half a mile wide, being long and narrow in form, as compared with other parks of equal size.

The narrow limits of this work utterly exclude the possibility of giving a detailed description of this magnificent enterprise; we, therefore, content ourselves by extracting from the celebrated manual of Mr. Valentine, the following general view:

"The most important improvement now being made in the city, is the regulation of the Central Park, which is situated very nearly in the geographical centre of the island, and comprises 773 acres, bounded by Fifty-ninth street, Fifth Avenue, 106th street, and Eighth Avenue. It is proposed to extend it to 110th street, in order to secure the very beautiful northern slope of a large hill, which lies mainly within the park. This extension will increase its size to about 840 acres. The receiving Croton Reservoir, and the new reservoir (now under construction) lie within the park, near its centre. The Central Park is to be, in all respects, as well adapted as is possible to the recreative wants of the people of the city; rich and poor, old and young, strong and weak, will here find common ground; and the arrangement of the various parts will be such as to afford the largest facilities for individual enjoyment, without interference from, or interfering with, those of different tastes. Pedestrians may roam at pleasure over twenty-five miles of walks, some fashionable and much frequented, others retired and quiet; or over hundreds of acres of lawn, woodland, and meadow. In their walks they may obtain any desirable observation of equipages and equestrians without once having to cross their track on the same level, or they may entirely seclude themselves, not only from the sight, but from the sound of vehicles. Riders on horseback may join the throng on the carriage-roads, or may confine their peregrinations to five miles of bridle road, on which no vehicle will be admitted. Nearly two miles of this ride will be about the new reservoir, where it is proposed to contrive for equestrians a level road forty feet in width. For carriages there will be nearly eight miles of broad, well-made roadway, affording, in its course, a view of nearly every object of interest in the Park, but nowhere crossing on the same level, a foot path of importance, or any portion of the bridle road. The main entrance to the Park will be at the corner of Fifth avenue and Fifty-ninth street, and there will be minor entrances at Seventh avenue—at either end of the Park—and at convenient points along Fifth and Eighth avenues. For the accommodation of business travel across the Park, there will be provided four transverse roads, so arranged as to pass under elevated portions of the roadways, and to afford a direct thoroughfare across the Park, without obstructing or being obstructed by pleasure travel. The prominent feature of the

Park will be a grand mall, one quarter of a mile in length, and two hundred feet in width, having a broad walk in its centre, and four rows of elm trees extending through its entire length. This mall will be approached at its southern end by a vestibule or lawn, ornamented with statuary, and it will terminate at its northern extremity in a richly decorated water terrace and fountain. At the foot of the terrace is the principal pond of the Park, containing nearly twenty acres of water, and skirting the Ramble—a rural promenading district south of the receiving reservoir. It was this pond which was filled for the benefit of skaters during the past winter."

Further and general information respecting the general features of the Park may be obtained from an admirable pamphlet entitled a "Guide to the Central Park," from which we extract the following:

HOW TO SEE THE PARK—CITY CARS.

The Central Park may be reached by the Third, Sixth, and Eighth avenue railroads. The Third avenue cars run from below the City Hall, near the Astor House, *via* the Bowery and Third avenue, to One Hundred and Thirtieth street, Harlem. This line runs parallel to the Park, two blocks distant, for its entire length, and affords the best accommodations for visiting those parts which are now most interesting. Passengers may leave the cars at the depot (Sixty-fifth street), and walk across Hamilton square and a partially open street, to the Fifth avenue, entering the Park at the Arsenal gate or at Sixty-seventh street, the route across being tolerable in dry weather; at Seventy-first street, which is open to a very favorable point of entrance; at Seventy-ninth street, on the upper side of which there is a good side-walk, to the Superintendent's office; at Eighty-sixth street, which is flagged to the Park, crossing it to the reservoirs; or at One Hundred and Ninth street, which is open to the Park near its northern boundary. These cars run every two and a half minutes, each alternate car (marked over the front "HARLEM AND YORKVILLE, DIRECT") running through to Harlem, and the others only to Sixty-fifth street. The fare to Sixty-fifth street is five cents; thence to

Harlem five cents; and through the entire route from the Astor House to Harlem, but six cents. The time from the Astor House to Sixty-fifth street is forty-eight minutes; to Seventy-ninth street, fifty-four minutes; to Ninety-second street, sixty minutes, and to Harlem, one hour and eighteen minutes. From Canal street it is eleven minutes less than from the Astor House, and from Fourteenth street, twenty-five minutes less. The Third avenue cars also run every few minutes to Sixty-fifth street, and two or three times an hour, to Harlem, all night.

The Sixth avenue cars run from the Astor House, and from Broadway and Canal street, *via* Varick street, etc., and the Sixth avenue, to Fifty-ninth street, the lower boundary of the Park. After leaving the cars, turn to the left, and enter at the first or second stile. The first leads to a high mass of rock, whence may be had a good view of that part of the park; and the second, by the easiest route to the drive.

The Eighth avenue cars start from the same points as the Sixth, and pass, *via* Hudson street, etc., to the Eighth avenue, on which they run to Forty-ninth street, whence passengers may walk, a half mile, to the park, or until they meet, at Fifty-first street (which they may, or may not), a small car, that runs to and from Fifty-ninth street. From the terminus of this line, one may turn to the right, and enter at the Seventh avenue gate, or continue up the Eighth avenue to the Sixty-second street gate. The fare on both of these roads is five cents, for any distance, and the cars run at frequent intervals.

A FEW WORDS ABOUT SOAP AND CANDLES.

————Industry,
To meditate, to plan, resolve, perform,
Which in itself is good—as surely brings
Reward of good, no matter what be done.
       POLLOK.

"The quantity of Soap consumed by a nation," says the celebrated Liebig in his familiar letters on chemistry, would be no inaccurate measure whereby to estimate its wealth and civilization. Political economists, indeed, will not give it this rank; but whether we regard it as joke or earnest, it is not the less true that, of two countries equal in population, we may declare with positive certainty, that the wealthiest and most highly civilized, is that which consumes the greatest weight of soap. It is not, however, merely by the quantity consumed of this important article, that the distinguished chemist would establish his claims to represent the civilization of a people. The vast train of chemical, manufacturing, and commercial operations called into existence for its economical production, and the cheaper, more extended, and altogether new arts and processes incidentally growing out of these, would, even with political economists, entitle it to this rank.

The materials used in making soaps are alkalies and fatty substances, or oils, both of animal and vegetable origin; of the former, potash, soda, and a small proportion of lime, are employed. The artificial production and cheap supply of soda from common salt, the alkali chiefly used, introduced about the beginning of the present century, has since that time completely revolutionized the business both in Europe and in this country, and probably within the last twenty years quadrupled the consumption of fats and oils. The principal ones used are, tallow and lard; palm, olive, and cocoa-nut oils. Rosin also enters largely into the composition of common yellow soap. Their chief agency is to serve as a vehicle for the alkali, upon which the detergent properties of soap mainly depend; while the combination of the latter with the fatty acids generated in the process of saponification, subdues its caustic qualities, and preserves the skin and the texture and colors of fabrics. Many other important and interesting facts relating to the manufacture of soap and candles might here be given, but want of space compels us to be brief; we therefore conclude our present article, by giving a practical illustration of the business.

J. C. HULL'S SON (Formerly Wager Hull & Son).

This house dates its existence as far back as 1780, having been established by a great-grandfather of the present firm, on a small lot of ground upon the present site. Since that period the business has passed through a succession of three generations, and is now in the hands of Charles Wager Hull, constituting an establishment of such great age, as is rarely to be found; and the fact of its remaining for such a length of time in the exclusive possession of one family, is one of the surest evidences of the thorough and practical knowledge of the business as conducted by the above-named firm.

The reputation for excellence which the soaps of this establishment have gained, is owing to the finer qualities of oils which are used, and which are entirely free from any injurious admixture of foreign substances so much used by many soap-makers to give strength to common soap, and to make cheaper any soap into which they are infused. In the production of fancy soaps, this establishment is not equalled by any other in the United States, comprising some seventy kinds, of all shapes, tints, stamps, sizes, and perfumes, and which in their appearance are truly beautiful and attractive. With reference to the candle department, it may be said, that candles are made here by a peculiar process, known only to this concern, and being made in large quantities, are offered to the trade at prices far below the mark elsewhere charged for articles of an inferior quality.

Were it necessary, we might enumerate some of the leading articles of Messrs. Hull's manufacture, which have gained great celebrity throughout the country; but they are so well-known, that eulogy would add nothing to the high appreciation in which they are already held. This being the oldest, and one of the largest and best-regulated soap and candle factories in the United States, it forms a matter of no surprise that its business is so largely and widely extended, reaching to the West Indies, and to South and Central America, and enjoying in our own country as well, a large share of patronage. Articles emanating from this establishment fully justify the correctness of the foregoing statements, and as experience is necessary to the production of perfect articles, it is to be presumed that a period of eighty-one years has not been spent in vain; hence it is that the oldest customers of the house have closely adhered to their first choice, while new ones, desiring to secure their own interests, are not slow to avail themselves of the advantages thus presented.

Among the articles for which the factory of J. C. Hull's Son has obtained a special and profitable celebrity, may be mentioned their *Pure Old Palm Soap*, which for many years they have manufactured to a large extent. It is made from pure palm oil, and is confessed equal to any imported article for the ordinary toilet purposes, for children, and for the bath. The known healing properties, peculiar to palm-oil, have made it highly valued, and especially adapt it for chapped hands in cold weather. We can recommend this truly excellent article, from long personal familiarity with it.

Notwithstanding its great merits, it is sold much lower than any imported soaps, and than many which are claimed to be imported. It has a slight, pleasing, delicate perfume; and, we should here observe that soaps are injured when too highly scented, although the uninformed in these matters are often led to imagine that the keener the odor the better the soap. J. C. Hull's Son likewise manufacture a very fine article of *Shaving Soap*, which we can commend for its quick and abundant lather, and its assistance to the razor in the smooth and easy removal of the beard.

Another article of their manufacture, which is of great importance and has come into extensive use for Railroads, Steamships, Mills, Machine shops, &c., is entitled *The Imperial Lubricating Oil*, and amongst its merits are the following: Its first cost is very much less than that of any other oil; all the gum in the oil is decomposed, so that it does not gum or clog up the journal or bearing; it keeps all journals cool, clean, and bright as new, so that they do not wear or tear, and thus much motive power is saved; it is free from any odor; it has great body, and so wears well, and thus, by its durability, it saves oil.

Conclusive testimonials as to these have been furnished to the public from the agents, inspectors, and engineers of some of the most extensive Railroads, Steamboats, Saw-Mills, Foundries, &c.; and to the Circular, containing these interesting and important communications, we refer the many who are interested. We have no doubt its extraordinary merits will enable it to supersede any other lubricating oil, and to be a great saving to all who shall use it.

Schieffelin Bros. & Co.

> Within the brain's most secret cells
> A certain lord-chief-justice dwells,
> Of sovereign power, whom, one and all,
> With common voice we Reason call.
>
> CHURCHILL.

The importation and manufacture of drugs and chemicals has become during the last half century among the most important and lucrative branches of business in America, and therefore deserves more than a passing notice.

A large proportion of the leading drugs used in the United States, are the products of foreign countries, and must be imported. The best antimony is imported from Hungary; assafœtida is the fetid concrete juice of a plant that grows in Persia; camphor comes from the East Indies and Japan; cassia from China; jalap is a Mexican plant, found near the city of Xalapa, after which it is named; the best opium is the juice of the white poppy, that grows in Turkey, Egypt, and the East Indies; hellebore is a native of the mountains of Switzerland and Germany; sarsaparilla is imported from South America, Honduras, and Quito; senna and scammony from Arabia; the best rhubarb from Asiatic Turkey, and so on through the whole genus, which it would be an endless task to particularize.

In the early stage of the drug business, these articles were solely imported by different merchants trading with the places where the various drugs were produced; but nearly a century ago the drug trade was made a specialty, although at the present day a large portion of our drugs are still brought into the market by the general merchant, or consigned to a commission house to sell on foreign account. These goods are generally sold through the drug broker, who sells the article as it is, and it requires good judgment and careful examination to buy advantageously in this matter, as many of the imported drugs and chemicals are adulterated by unscrupulous foreign manufacturers expressly for this market, in order to undersell the honest trade. To such an extent was this adulteration carried on a few years ago, that the New York College of Pharmacy published an analysis of the composition of some well-known articles, from which, by way of example, we extract the following:—"An imported blue pill contains a percentage of mercury from ten down to seven and a half, mixed with blue clay and Prussian blue to give the proper design and color. Its composition, according to Prof. Reid, is mercury, earthy clay, Prussian blue, sand in combination with the clay, soluble saccharine matters, insoluble organic matter and water. Very large quantities of rhubarb much decayed, the better parts of which are dark colored, with scarcely any taste or smell, having probably been exhausted to make extracts, come from England at very low prices. It is intended and used for powdering, color being given by turmeric, &c. Most of the foreign extracts are not what they profess to be, and cannot be relied upon in the treatment of disease." We could multiply these examples to an indefinite extent, but the above will be sufficient to show the extent of the evil, the effectual remedy to which can only be found in the improved knowledge and culture of the buyers, and above all in purchasing at fair prices from importers of known integrity, and drug houses who make drugs, chemicals, and druggists' articles their specialty.

The house whose name heads this article, Messrs. Schieffelin Brothers & Co., William street, corner of Beekman, New York, is one of the oldest, and, we believe, the leading drug importing house in the United States. Established for three generations, having a large capital and great experience, this firm is able to compete on the one hand with the most favored in the markets of Europe, and on the other to distribute the articles of their importation through wholesale druggists throughout the country. They have furthermore the advantage of having experienced agents located in the drug-producing countries, whose instructions are to purchase and ship direct none but the *best* and *purest* qualities. Thus as they sell what they import direct from their own stores, the superiority of their importations may be as confidently asserted as they are generally acknowledged.

To give a better idea of the ramifications of the trade of this house throughout the globe, we subjoin a partial list of the places where their agents are located, being London, Liverpool, Northampton, Cork, Glasgow, Amsterdam, Rotterdam, Antwerp, Paris, Lyons, Marseilles, Grasse, Montpelier, Nimes, Dresden, Berlin, Darmstadt, Leghorn, Genoa, Penang, Naples, Trieste, Messina, Smyrna, Constantinople, Alexandria, Egypt, St. Petersburg, Bombay, Calcutta, Singapore, Penang, Batavia, Canton, Shanghai, Manilla, Colombo, and various places in South America. Thus laying three continents under contribution for their balms to heal the sick, their dye stuffs and pigments for the mechanic arts, their spices for the epicure, and their thousand and one extracts and essences for all conceivable purposes.

The drug trade during the last few years has not only vastly increased, but has also undergone a vast change in the stock required to be kept on hand. Not only is it now necessary to keep crude drugs, chemicals, and essential oils, but a perfect stock must comprise these, and also medicines, essences, extracts, oils, paints, dye stuffs, and druggists' wares; and still more recently another branch has been introduced, that of keeping on hand foreign and domestic perfumery, toilet articles, India-rubber goods, instruments, and fancy goods generally, of all of which Messrs. S. B. & Co. have always a large stock on hand, suitable for jobbers, which we purpose more particularly detailing in the following brief description of their premises, which we had the privilege of inspecting a few days ago.

The building has a frontage on William street of eighty eight feet, running back on Beekman street seventy-two feet. It is six stories high, with basement and sub-cellar, built of pressed brick in the most substantial manner, which is necessary to enable it to bear the immense weight nearly always contained in it. The fourth, fifth, and sixth floors are crowded with whole packages of non-combustible goods, and each floor has one man whose special business it is to attend to it, to receive and deliver goods through the hatchways, of which there are two, and to keep them in proper order, by which means every article is kept in its place, and can be immediately had when wanted.

The third floor is divided into two parts; one for open packages, mortars, glass, slabs, and druggists' ware. The other is for patent medicines, Shakers, and other herbs, and such like, each under the charge of a separate foreman, one of whom has been with the firm over twenty-nine years.

The second story is used for putting up goods, and is divided into three compartments under one superintendent. The first is the city department, for putting up all orders for the city retail trade; the second department is the oil and liquid room, where all goods for bottles or cans are put up; while the third is used for filling country orders. This floor is a constant scene of activity, yet with all the vast amount of work that has to be done, owing to the admirable system which prevails, neither here nor in any other part of the house, notwithstanding there are sixty men employed, is there the slightest bustle or confusion. Everything moves like clock-work, in perfect order.

Descending to the basement, we find piles of dye stuffs, gums, &c., and other like articles, while on the William street front is situated the sponge room, containing all kinds and qualities, from the grass sponge of the Bahamas, to the finer qualities imported from Smyrna, Turkey, and Trieste, ranging from seven cents to forty dollars per pound. This is a most valuable stock, and it is believed Messrs. S. B. & Co. have the largest in the country. Passing from here under the sidewalk, which is lighted by means of the patent vault lights, our olfactories give notice that we are approaching the extracts and essences, which are ranged in a series of strongly built vaults to protect them from heat, where are also kept the essential oils, opium, &c. Turning round on the Beekman street side are another series of vaults containing all the combustible articles, such as ether, oil of vitriol, and other acids, none of which articles are ever allowed in the main building.

Descending once again to the lowest deep, we come upon a miscellaneous assortment of heavy articles, such as soda, salæratus, salts, &c. Here also are the two steam engines for hoisting, and heating the building, the boilers supplying the steam being under the sidewalk, which is the only place where any fire throughout the whole building is allowed. There are also another range of vaults, where the balance of inflammable or explosive articles are kept.

We now come to the first floor, which, though last, is not least. Entering from the corner, you come into a spacious room, on the left of which are a series of desks and partitions appropriated for the bookkeeper, cashier, and assistants.

In the centre and right are a series of desks occupied by the members of the firm and the buyers and salesmen of the different departments, whilst at the end is an office devoted for the reception of customers or others having private business with the house. Beyond this, separated by a partition, is the shipping room, where all goods are received and shipped. This room extends the whole width of the building, with an entrance on Beckman street, and during the busy season is a scene of incessant activity. On the other side, with an entrance on William street, is the sample room and fancy goods department. But it would be an endless task to enumerate these. We can only give the principal headings :—Perfumery, foreign and domestic, of all the best brands, toilet articles, &c.; brushes, artists' marking, painters', pencil, toilet, &c., of all conceivable styles and qualities ; combs, buff, horn, ivory, India-rubber, &c.; instruments, physicians' articles, trusses, syringes, &c.; India-rubber goods of every description ; chemists' and druggists' pottery and glassware, furniture articles, mortars, &c.; druggists' sundries, boxes, bronzes, flasks, glaziers' diamonds, drug mills and tincture presses, inks, mirrors, tube and toy paints, pencils, pill machines, soda water appurtenances, scales and weights, chamois, split, and plaster skins, lint, corks, in fact every article that is required for the perfect fitting up of a retail drug store.

We may also mention that they are the sole agents of *Beranger's French Balances*, universally admitted to be the most correct, durable, and elegant scales yet invented.

This imperfect sketch conveys but a very faint idea of the magnitude of the business of the house, but the facilities they possess for buying in the producing countries, joined to their large capital and great practical knowledge, give them advantages few in the trade have.

A machine which will make 100,000 slate pencils a day, has been invented by a Hartford, Ct., mechanic.

SALÆRATUS, BI-CARB. SODA, CREAM TARTAR, YEAST POWDER.

> He that neglects a blessing, though he want
> No present knowledge how to use it,
> Neglects himself.
>
> BEAUMONT AND FLETCHER.

ANDREWS & CO., 136 & 138 CEDAR STREET, NEW YORK.

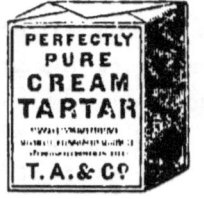

There is nothing like a spirit of enterprise and an accommodating good will, to secure business and prosperity. They always procure the best of friends, and while the slow, careless, and unamiable man is left behind, the active, persevering, and courteous one distances all competition.

Mr. Thomas Andrews, of this city, is a case in point. This gentleman's career has been characterized by a degree of prosperity seldom, if ever, attained by one so young in years. From an unusually low station in life, until as a printer's boy he attained his first education, he has gradually advanced in mercantile life, through numberless trials and difficulties, by strict probity, self-denial, and economy, until he stands at the head of a new and important branch of trade—the largest of its kind in the Union.

Some fourteen years since, Mr. Andrews originated in a small way, the supplying of Wholesale Grocers with Bi-Carb. Soda, Cream Tartar, and Sal Soda, which articles were in light demand by that trade, being sold almost exclusively by druggists. This succeeded, and he originated and introduced for another firm Saleratus in one pound papers. This was also adopted by the whole trade, and became universal.

Mr. Andrews then pushed out on his own account, and met

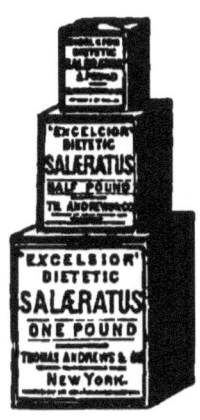

with the most unscrupulous opposition from those whom interest arrayed against him, and after stemming the tide for eight years alone, associated with him Mr. George F. Gantz, whose mercantile education was acquired in the house of H. M. Schieffelin & Fowler. And thus the firm is at present constituted. About six years since this firm erected the Jersey City Chemical works, opposite New York.

These were constructed for the manufacture of Saleratus, Bi-Carb. Soda for Refining Ash, &c., at a cost of $35,000. They occupy seven lots, and possess facilities for refining and carbonizing thirty tons per week, which is the average product of these works.

The stores and office of this house in this city are at 136 and 138 Cedar street, known as the "Excelsior" Steam Mills, where an extensive business is transacted. Thomas Andrews & Co. are largely engaged in the importation and jobbing of the finest grades of Bi-Carb. Soda, Cream Tartar, Soda Ash, Sal Soda, Canstic Soda, &c. Of Bi-Carb. Soda, their sales have reached 30,000 kegs per annum ; of Sal Soda, their sales average 25 tons per week; and of Cream Tartar, perfectly pure, their sales average 1,000 pounds per

THE UNION SKETCH BOOK.

day. Of the article of Yeast Powder, they dispose of over 200,000 tins per annum. This "demand speaks for itself," as their goods give universal satisfaction. The amount of cash capital required for this large trade is over $75,000, while the regular sales do not fall short of half a million of dollars annually. This much can be said of this house, they have always studied the interest of their jobbing customers, and have never interfered with retail trade.

The following comprises the lines of goods sold by this firm:—

"Golden Rule," "Paragon," and Excelsior Salæratus (the Best Dietetic), Pure Double Refined, and Soda Salæratus, the various qualities of which are put up in every conceivable style, the name of any firm inserted on the labels and boxes. By this method jobbers circulate their own name to their own trade.

Thomas Andrews' Excelsior Yeast Powder has superseded nearly all the various preparations intended for the effectual raising of bread, biscuit, &c. It is universally admired, and is perfectly healthy and dietetic.

Bi-Carbonate Soda, the best Newcastle brands, in papers or boxes, or by 10 to 1,000 kegs, in store or to arrive. Also the "Frear's Goose," made by the Jersey City Chemical Works, sold at a less price than foreign, and warranted to give satisfaction.

Perfectly pure Cream Tartar, prepared under the personal supervision of the firm. No impurity in this valuable article is permitted. For medical or family use, the Cream Tartar from this house is unrivalled in its reputation.

This firm has the largest stock of different brands and tests of Soda Ash, Caustic Soda, &c. Agents of the Penn. Salt Co. Concentrated Lye, Soap Powder, Castile Soap, Prepared Pot Ash, Pot and Pearl Ashes, Indigo, Saltpetre, Tartaric Acid, Rice Flour, &c. All these articles guaranteed.

That a business to the extent done by the above firm should grow out of nothing but good judgment, tact, and perseverance, shows what can be accomplished in any department of trade, combined with strict integrity and straightforward dealing.

Remember the house of Thomas Andrews and Co., New York, when writing out your order.

CULTIVATED WOMEN.—Sheridan said, beautifully, "Women govern us; let us render them perfect. The more they are enlightened, so much the more shall we be. On the cultivation of the mind of women depends the wisdom of men. It is by women that nature writes on the hearts of men."

TIN WARE.

> Let not one look of fortune cast you down;
> She were not fortune if she did not frown:
> Such as do bravcliest bear scorns awhile,
> Are those on whom at last she most will smile.
>
> LORD ORRERY.

The annexed engraving represents J. D. Locke's manufactory of PLAIN, JAPANNED, STAMPED and PLANISHED tin ware. The idea of an establishment for the manufacture and sale of tin ware is almost invariably associated in the mind of the general public with the outside display of a number of articles of tin and iron; a few broken stoves on the sidewalk; a dingy, dirty back workshop, containing sundry piles of metals, a quantity of dirty benches, with numerous queer-looking machines and tools lying about promiscuously, finishing off with a sign outside of —————, manufacturer of stoves, tin-ware, &c., with a P. S., Jobbing attended to, and pots and kettles to mend. Such was formerly the appearance of many of the trade; but the requirements of the age and the enterprise of our manufacturers have changed all this now. About ten or twelve years ago planished tin-ware was but little known in this country as a branch of manufacture, our dealers being then entirely dependent on the European market for their supplies; at present we can manufacture this class of goods equal in quality and fineness of finish to the English, and at a far less cost.

To give an idea of the extent the business has attained, we will give a few statistics connected with this House. Mr. J. D. Locke has been about thirty-four years in the business; some eight or nine years ago he built the main building, at Whitestone, Long Island, since which he has been making continual additions to it to meet the requirements of his increased trade, and as the results of his enterprise, system, and strict attention to business, he has been enabled to keep his whole force of workmen, consisting of 125 to 150 hands, fully employed all the past winter, and during the present dull times. His annual consumption of tin is about 8000 boxes, manufactured into all conceivable articles that this metal can be used for; the catalogue of these contains 130 pages, of which we propose giving a synopsis.

Twenty-five pages enumerate fifty-three different articles of japanned tin-ware, divided into hundreds of sizes and varieties. Fifteen pages are devoted to the description of forty-five articles of stamped ware, equally diverse in size and shape; two pages to lamp trimmings, and two to the varieties of tea-trays and waiters. We next come to tin-ware proper occupying twelve pages, enumerating thirty different articles, with almost ten times thirty different varieties. French-tinned goods of all descriptions occupy four pages more. Planished tin-ware embracing twenty-seven different articles occupies twelve pages; while tinmen's tools and machines, occupying thirteen pages, enumerate everything required by them in the business. Of these latter articles the manufacturer in this catalogue says : "These machines are made of the *best* materials that can be obtained, and in the *best* manner, with brass-wheels, top-plates, and boxes with all the present improvements, to which will be added every real improvement that can be made." The remaining forty pages of the catalogue are taken up with the enumeration of the immense variety of articles comprised under the headings of, hollow-ware, housekeeping hardware, silver-plated ware, Britannia ware, spoons, rolled metal, castors, frames, lamps and candlesticks, ladles, beer-mugs, spittoons, &c. &c.

From this brief resumé some idea of the present extent of

this business may be formed, and those interested in it will readily appreciate the labor required to bring it to such perfection. Mr. J. D. Locke has removed his warehouse from the old stand in Water street to more commodious premises, at No. 47 Cliff street (between Beekman and Fulton), New York, where dealers will find as complete a stock as capital, enterprise, and skill can produce, to be purchased on as advantageous terms as any in the market.

NOTHING LIKE LEATHER.—At a public sale of books, the auctioneer put up Drew's " Essay on Souls," which was knocked down to a shoemaker, who very innocently, but to the great amusement of the crowded room, asked the auctioneer if " he had any more works on shoemaking to sell."

YOUNG'S NIGHT THOUGHTS.—" The title of my poem, Night Thoughts," says Dr. Young, " is not affected, for I never compose but at night, except sometimes when on horseback."

AN exhibition of pictures by modern artists has recently been opened in Manchester, England, and among them are 246 works by French, English, and German artists : there were two by Decamps, the celebrated French artist, which were painted just previous to his death ; but there are no American names mentioned among the artists who contribute the works for the exhibition.

Brave men bare their bosoms to their enemies; fashionable women to friends and enemies alike.

PARKS.

The Battery, fronting the harbor.

The City Hall Park.

St. John's Park, fronting St. John's Church, and bounded by Hudson, Varick, Beach, and Laight streets.

Washington Square is bounded by Waverley place, M'Dougal, Fourth, and Wooster streets.

Tompkins Square, formerly a military parade-ground, is on the eastern side of the city, and is bounded by avenues A and B, and by 6th and 10th streets.

Union Park is a beautiful oval area, at the head of Broadway, bounded by University place (which is called a continuation of Broadway, at the Park), the 4th avenue, and 14th and 17th streets. Adjoining this park stands the Equestrian Statue of Washington.

Stuyvesant Square, in front of the new St. George's church, is between 15th and 17th streets.

Gramercy Park, bounded by 20th and 21st streets, and lying between Third and Fourth avenues.

Madison Square, bounded by Fifth and Madison avenues, and 23d and 26th streets.

Hamilton Square, between the Third and Fifth avenues, and 68th and 69th streets.

Bloomingdale Square is between the Eighth and Ninth avenues, and 53d and 57th streets.

Manhattan Square, between the Eighth and Ninth avenues, and bounded by 77th and 81st streets.

Mount Morris, near Harlem, a rocky elevation in the centre of a public square, between 120th and 124th streets, and extending on each side of the Fifth avenue.

Central Park, bounded by Fifth and Eighth avenues, and 59th and 106th streets.

High Bridge, 173d street, eleven miles from the City Hall.

Croton Reservoir, bounded by 79th and 86th streets, and the 6th and 7th avenues.

New Receiving Reservoir, located within the Central Park, fronting on 5th avenue, extending from 86th to 96th streets, and contains 112 acres.

RAILROAD DEPOTS.

Albany and intermediate Places, *via* Hudson river railroad; Chambers street, c. Hudson; Canal street, c. West, and 31st street, n. 10th avenue.

Albany and Intermediate Places, *via* Harlem railroad; 26th street and 4th avenue, and Centre c. White street.

Boston, Dunkirk, and the West, *via* Erie railroad, foot of Duane street.

Boston, *via* Fall River; steamboat route to Fall River, where the railroad commences.

Boston, *via* Stonington and Providence; steamboat route, from foot of Vestry street to Allen's Point, n. Norwich, thence by railroad.

Boston, *via* New Haven and Hartford; 27th street and 4th avenue.

Easton; by ferry, from foot of Cortlandt street to Jersey city, where the railroad commences.

Greenpoint, and all the places on Long Island, from South ferry, Brooklyn.

Newark, Paterson, and Morristown railroads, foot of Cortlandt street.

Philadelphia, Washington, and all southern and southwestern

places; foot of Cortlandt street ferry to Jersey city, thence by railroad.

Philadelphia, *via* South Amboy; by steamer from Battery to South Amboy, thence by railroad.

CITY RAILROADS.

Harlem, Fourth Avenue Railroad, from Astor House through Centre, Grand, Bowery, 4th avenue, to East 27th street.

Second Avenue Railroad, from Peck slip through Pearl, Chatham, Bowery, Grand, Allen streets, 1st avenue, East 23d street, 2d avenue, to Harlem; returning, through 2d avenue, Chrystie, Grand, Bowery, Chatham, Oliver, South streets, to Peck slip.

Third Avenue Railroad, from Astor House through Park row, Chatham, Bowery, 3d avenue to Harlem, returning same route.

Sixth Avenue Railroad, from Barclay street, through Church, Chambers, West Broadway, Canal, Varick, Carmine streets, 6th avenue, to West 44th street, returning the same way.

Eighth Avenue Railroad, from Barclay street, through Church, Chambers, West Broadway, Canal, Hudson streets, 8th avenue, to West 54th street, returning the same route.

☞ Fare on all the roads through the city 5 cents. On 2d and 3d avenue roads, to Harlem, 6 cents.

Of 50,000 PERSONS insured in the London (Eng.) Accidental Death Insurance Company, 22 were seriously injured by falls on street slides in the course of a single fortnight. Three adults are suffering with broken legs and two with severe spinal injuries, the result of idle boys sliding on sidewalks.

ROOFING.

> Labor is rest—from the sorrows that greet us,
> Rest from all petty vexations that meet us,
> Rest from sin-promptings that ever entreat us,
> Rest from world-syrens that lure us to ill.
> Mrs. Osgood.

The rapid increase of the population of large cities, and the still more incredible increase of the population, by immigration and otherwise, of these United States, has formed an incentive for our people to exercise their inventive genius in supplying this increase with the necessary food, clothing, and habitations, by means of improved machinery and inventions suitable to meet the increased wants as fast as they arise. Amongst these new inventions must be classed, as a very important item, the article of roofing. Shingle roofs were amongst the first used; earthen tiles may be classed next, and then slate and tin; after which, as a modern invention, comes the gravel roof. Now all these roofs were, and are still, useful in their way, but they none of them combine all the qualities requisite in a roof, the three most important of which are, first, to be perfectly fire and waterproof; secondly, not to be liable to injury from either heat or cold; thirdly, to be economic in cost; and, lastly, to be durable and easily adapted to all kinds of roofs. It was reserved for this generation to discover the means of combining all these objects in one.

Some four years ago Messrs. Johns & Crosley, then of Brooklyn, afterwards of 510 Broadway, since removed, and at present at 78 William street, New York, discovered the means of forming a roof for any kind of building that should be fireproof, water-proof, time-proof, light, economic, and easily put on by any mechanic. It is essentially, as its name implies, a

Gutta-Percha Cement Roofing, being composed of gutta-percha and india-rubber, combined together with various other ingredients, forming a chemical combination unequalled by any article for similar purposes ever produced. This Gutta-Percha Cement—in liquid form—has been proved to be the cheapest and most durable coating for metals of all kinds of any paint or composition in use, and for *Tin and Metal Roofs* of all kinds it is invaluable. At first the public were incredulous as to its qualities, as they generally are of most new inventions; but by degrees their prejudice wore away, as they began to experience the benefit of it by actual trial, until at the present time it is recognised as an indispensability; and as a further proof of the favor it has attained, we may mention that they have applied it to over three thousand buildings of various kinds in this city and vicinity alone, and are also constantly receiving orders for it from all parts of the United States, the Canadas, the West Indies, and South America, whilst thousands of dollars' worth of property have been saved by its fire-proof qualities. So steadily and constantly has the demand been increasing that they have been compelled to enlarge their factory in Brooklyn three several times, until at the present moment it covers over two acres of ground, and Messrs. Johns & Crosley are now reaping the benefit of the invention which cost them so much time and labor to perfect.

The Roofing consists of a Water-Proof Roofing Cloth, combined with a first quality Roofing Felt, saturated with a composition of Gutta-Percha and India-Rubber, which not only preserves the cloth, but renders it in the highest degree elastic, so that shrinking of new roof boards will not injure it. This is to be nailed to roof boards, or directly to old shingle roofs, and then coated and finished with the Gutta-Percha Cement (a sufficient quantity of which is always sent with the cloth to finish the roof), and sanded as per directions; thus giving a surface of stone and at the same time an elastic body. This material forms a perfectly water-tight roof as soon as applied, which is not the case with the generality of composition roofs, it being necessary with them to apply two or three coats of paint, and wait four or five days for each coat to dry, thus occasioning a great loss of time, and unnecessary labor and expense.

The Roofing is furnished complete, and prepared ready for use (with full printed instructions for application), to those who wish to apply it themselves for about one-third the price of tin.

The expense of applying it is trifling, as an ordinary roof can be covered and finished the same day.

Such is a slight description and review of the qualities of this improved roofing material. Should any party desire further information respecting it, Messrs. Johns & Crosley will gladly furnish it on application at their store, 78 William street, where they also will be happy to show the numerous testimonials they have received from the various parties who have this roofing now in use.

Messrs. Johns & Crosley are also sole manufacturers of the AMERICAN CEMENT GLUE, a most useful article, and the only glue ever manufactured that will withstand water, for cementing wood, glass, ivory, leather, china, marble, porcelain, alabaster, bone, coral, &c., &c. It is highly spoken of by families using it.

Everybody knows the comfort of a spring bed. Messrs. Johns & Crosley have the agency of Ulmer's Patent Spring Bed Bottom, one of the most ingenious and cheapest luxuries of the age. It was patented in October, 1859, and is much appreciated by those using it for its qualifications, amongst which may be classed the following :

First. It is simple, and easily understood.

Second. Any person can put them up, it being only necessary to saw the end strip the necessary length, and screw it to the bedstead.

Third. For comfort, ease, and elasticity it is not excelled by any other bed bottom.

Fourth. Not easily getting out of repair, it is durable, and will last a lifetime.

Fifth. It will fit any bedstead, by merely adjusting the ends of the slats and end strips—a frame not being necessary.

Sixth. You can arrange the head so that it will be higher than the foot; and when in use it is perfectly noiseless.

Seventh. Once on, vermin will not live in them, the vulcanized rubber driving them away.

Eighth. Only one mattress is necessary.

Ninth. They are the cheapest bed bottom in the market, being sold from Three Dollars and Fifty Cents to Five Dollars.

Tenth. By reason of these facts they are a commercial article. They are packed in such a small compass, and cost so little for freight, that they can become an article of trade.

Messrs. Johns & Crosley are now prepared to establish agencies for the sale of this patent all over the United States and Canadas, and invite country merchants to call on them and inspect it at their warehouse, 78 William street, New York.

It is well known that several species of fish may be frozen quite stiff, carried several miles, and when put into cold water they will revive. Several artificial ponds have been stocked with fish carried from a distance in a frozen state; and yet it is stated that the celebrated Dr. John Hunter, having tried several experiments to restore frozen fish, always failed to do so. A recent French experimenter in this line states that he has discovered the reason of this. He asserts that the tissues of fish and frogs may be frozen and the creatures may be restored to activity, but if their *hearts* become ice-chilled they never can be reanimated.

BILLIARDS.

> What is title? what is treasure?
> What is reputation's care?
> If we lead a life of pleasure,
> 'Tis no matter how or where.
>
> BURNS.

Throughout the entire range of elegant amusements there is none which, in the average of general excellence and the number of faculties both physical and mental which it calls into play, can compete with the game of billiards. That amusement is certainly the best, the most pleasurable, which occupies, that is to say *amuses*, the greatest number of organs and facul-

ties at one time, to a point which fully exercises without straining or fatiguing them. As a practical illustration of our assertion, let us consider certain popular amusements and the relative play they give to the various portions of the player's organization. The game of ten-pins, for instance, calls into requisition the physical qualities merely, and even then not all of them. Quoits are on a par with ten-pins. Both of these games soon cease to be amusing, for neither of them supplies amusement for the mental faculties; and as these faculties, in a man of properly developed intellect, are the most imperative in their demands for occupation or entertainment, the game which ignores them ceases any longer to be amusing when the need of physical exercise is no longer pressing, and the stimulus of a mental direction is lacking.

The game of billiards requires the lively, continuous, and

intelligent exercise of the various groups of intellectual organs, and a promptness, decision, vivacity, and steadiness in the physical machinery to carry out the conceptions of the mind. The intellect is kept in healthy exercise by the continual demand upon it for rapid combinations to meet the various exigencies caused by the ever changing and ever new positions of the balls. The eye is kept continually at work, rapidly estimating distances, taking points, and describing angles, and enabling the mind to judge the momentum necessary to be applied to the ball for the production of desired results. The arm must instinctively recognise what the mind requires of it, and rapidly and exactly execute it. All the faculties are kept in continuous play; every muscle has its share in the game. The left hand has its office to perform as well as the right; the dorsal column is extended, ployed, curved; the legs have their full share of work. Billiards, then, exercising as it does, to a higher average degree than any amusement yet invented, both the mental and physical qualities of our organization, combining the intellectual and the material in the relative ratio which they should hold to each other in a well balanced organization, is, in our opinion, the first of amusements—the amusement most befitting "a well balanced organization," that is, a complete man.

The game of billiards, according to all historical probabilities, is of French origin, but in no country in the world is it played to the same extent as in the United States. In fact, so universal has it become among us that it may now be called, *par excellence*, the American national amusement. Its peculiar excellences, its happy combination of the scientific and the mechanical, the contemplative and the constructive, especially recommend it to the particular idiosyncrasy of the American. It is a remarkable fact that while we probably owe the invention to France, and the vast improvements in the machinery of the game are of American-origin, England has made no contribution to its furtherance of perfection in any way, and billiards is still played in the latter country in the same plodding way in which it was played by the old English gentlemen some sixty years ago. The machinery of the game has reached its highest degree of perfection in this country. It was completely revolutionized some seven years since by MICHAEL PHELAN's admirable invention—the combination cushion, and the various improvements in shape, style, &c., since made by that gentleman, to whom all lovers of scientific billiards owe a debt of lasting gratitude. These cushions, which have been patented and universally adopted in this country, and for which a patent has also been granted by the French government, at once obviated all the inconveniences of the old style cushions, their incorrectness of angle, their liability to variation from atmospheric changes, &c., and made billiards almost an exact science. Mr. PHELAN not only effected a material revolution in billiards; he accomplished their moral and social elevation. He convinced the public that billiards was not a game for loafers or blacklegs, but for ladies and gentlemen; and it is, in the main, to his exertions the fact is due that the billiard table has now become a domestic institution, and billiards the favorite amusement of the cultivated of both sexes.

PHELAN's Model Table, with Combination Cushions, is manufactured solely by Messrs. PHELAN & COLLENDER, at their extensive manufactory, 63, 65, and 67 Crosby street. The manufactory is by far the most extensive and complete establishment of the kind in the world. It is five stories in height, seventy-five feet front, and one hundred feet deep. From roof to foundation, every portion of the immense building is occupied with the various operations connected with the diverse articles of billiard manufacture. Every operation is performed by the newest inventions in machinery, worked by a steam-engine of twenty-six horse power, built expressly for the firm. The basement, which is well adapted to the purpose, is used exclusively for marble work. Here the beds for tables are formed and polished. The first or main floor is the exhibition and salesroom, where at all times may be found a great variety of tables finished in various styles, which, in point of exquisite beauty of workmanship, cannot be equalled. Connecting with this floor also are two offices, both of which are neatly furnished and tastefully arranged. The second floor is the fitting room, where the various parts of the tables are put together. Above this is the machinery room, where can be seen a large amount of useful and valuable machinery, such as planing, sawing, tenoning, mortising, and moulding machines. The fourth floor is the veneering room, provided with a steam apparatus for veneering. The fifth floor is the varnishing and finishing room. Connecting with the principal workshops are adjoining rooms, used for such purposes as painting, making cushions, &c. The establishment throughout is complete in every respect, affording the proprietors every opportunity for the manufacture of tables on the most extensive scale.

All the various articles of billiard machinery are to be found at the Phelan Factory. Among the novelties lately introduced by Messrs. PHELAN & COLLENDER are the Self-adhesive Cue Leathers, prepared so that they can be put on the cue as easily as a postage-stamp on a letter, dispensing with screws, glue, or cue-wax.

THE way to render amusements innocuous is not by violent prohibition of them, but by surrounding them with such chastening and refining influences that they shall lose all tendency to evil.

SHIP BREAD AND CRACKERS.

> Let us then be up and doing,
> With a heart for every fate;
> Still achieving, still pursuing,
> Learn to labor and to wait.
>
> LONGFELLOW.

HOW OUR SOLDIERS AND SAILORS ARE FED.

Everybody, we expect, has often noticed in passing through the streets of our cities the signs of "Ship Bread and Cracker Bakeries," but few, we doubt, have ever had the curiosity to inspect the interior of them, nor have the large majority a very clear idea of the amount of ingenious machinery employed in this important branch of industry; and we might go even farther and say, that to most it will be news to learn that nearly the whole of the vast quantity of bread required for our Army, Navy, Volunteers, and mercantile marine, is made almost entirely by machinery, little or no manipulation being required in its manufacture, and that little, merely as guides and aids to the machinery.

We recently had the pleasure of inspecting one of the largest establishments of the kind in New York, or in fact in the country, which we propose in the present article describing, prefacing it, however, with a slight review of the early history of the House, for although a business of colossal magnitude at the present day, it was not so in its earlier stages.

Ephraim Treadwell's Sons is the present title of the firm; the partners being Wm. E. Treadwell, Wm. Hustace, and Chas. J. Harris. The father of W. E. T—, Ephraim Treadwell, founded the establishment in 1820, in Dey street, between Greenwich and Washington streets. At that time the business, being small, consuming but about five barrels of flour daily, the work was then altogether done by hand labor. Several machinists at this period turned their attention to the invention of machinery for the use of cracker bakers, and E. T. was among the first to encourage the introduction of the then novelty. Any new machine that promised to save labor and to attain the desired end, was always carefully investigated, and if the trial proved satisfactory, was certainly adopted by him. In this way, by constantly studying all the new inventions that came under his notice, and being naturally of a mechanical turn of mind, he by degrees invented several valuable improvements, amongst which, as the most important and useful, may be mentioned an improvement in the cutting machine, and two more valuable ones in the arrangement of ovens, one of which, patented in 1853, the present firm has now in use. In 1829 they removed to the corner of Warren and Washington streets, where they still continue manufacturing at this establishment the finer qualities of crackers, such as Sugar, Boston, Oyster, and Water crackers, and Soda, Milk, Wine, Maple, Extra Butter, and Abernethy biscuits. It was here that steam power was first introduced into the business, the new motor and increased power being required to supply the demand which had increased from the daily consumption of five barrels of flour in 1820 to fifty barrels in 1840. In June, 1853, they had again to look for further facilities to enable them to fill their orders, and engaged the premises No. 244 Front street, where they now manufacture the largest part of the ship bread and crackers, such as are required for the use of the army, navy, and mercantile marine. This increase has probably given them larger manufacturing facilities than any other establishment, as they are now using in their two factories about *two hundred barrels of flour daily*.

Two hundred barrels of flour, each containing one hundred and ninety-six lbs., to be made up into crackers and biscuits of all conceivable shapes, forms, and sizes in one day! We confess to know little or nothing of the mysteries of the culinary, confectionery, or bakery arts and sciences, but we have a pretty vivid recollection of having at times seen a few pounds of flour converted into bread, cakes, pies, puddings, etc., all of which took a long time to perform; and judging from our experience in this respect, we could scarcely realize how the said two hundred barrels of thirty-nine thousand two hundred lbs. of flour could be converted into good wholesome bread in twelve hours, but we have now seen it all, and will try to describe the process for the benefit of those who may not have been as fortunate. As an illustration, let us take the ship bread establishment at 244 Front street. This building is five stories high, about twenty-seven feet front, and ninety feet deep, and has been constructed expressly for the purpose of the business. All the fire required for the boilers and ovens, or heating purposes, is in the basement, and to prevent any possibility of danger from this source, the floor and ceiling covering it is composed of iron girders arched in with brick covered with cement and then planked, forming a compact fire-proof flooring. Passing from the front to the rear of the first floor, we come to the mixing room, on either side of which are two immense troughs, in which the ingredients are poured for forming the dough. Here a skilful workman is required—it being most essential to have the dough the exact consistency; when this is attained it is passed up an inclined plane into a box, where some very beautiful machinery thoroughly kneads it and passes it through a receiver to the floor below; the mass then passes through a pair of rollers and comes out a thick sheet of dough; from here it is carried by hand to another set of rollers gauged to flatten it to the exact thickness required; these rollers deliver a continued sheet of dough about eighteen inches in width on to a revolving band which carries it forward to the cutting machine, but previous to getting there it requires a little dry flour which the machine dredges over it on its passage, and that it may be perfectly distributed, a set of brushes are made to revolve back and forth over it. The cutting machinery contains the dies that mark, shape, and cut the crackers the required form, rising and falling at the same speed as the dough progresses, and at each motion cutting, marking, and shaping from twelve to twenty crackers. In the case of round crackers or ship bread, the surplus dough is gathered up by a boy as it passes to the end of the revolving band, where the bread is dexterously caught on a board and carried to the oven. So rapidly are all these operations performed that it requires one man's constant attention to catch and remove the bread to the oven, a distance of only some few feet.

The oven is one of the most perfect and ingenious pieces of mechanism ever invented. The external structure is of brickwork, forty-two feet long, twelve feet wide, and ten feet high. The heat is applied by means of hot air flues, of which there are sixteen, and this heat is furnished by two furnaces in the front of the oven: the first furnace supplies the eight flues which run at the lower part of the oven, and the second one the eight in the upper part; by this arrangement the same heat is applied to the upper as to the lower part of the bread to be baked, thus insuring an evenness of baking on both sides.

What is generally understood as the bottom of the oven when stationary, but what in this case is known as the baking surface, consists of an *endless* perforated wire-band extending the whole width and length of the oven, and then passing over cylinders which are kept revolving by steam power. There is an entrance at one end of the oven in which the bread is placed, and it requires one man to be very active to keep it supplied; it then passes slowly, the speed being regulated according to the requirements of the style of bread being baked, to the other end of the oven, where stands the foreman of the establishment with a monstrous rake drawing it from the oven into large baskets as fast as it arrives. The foreman is stationed here, as it requires a man of experience to know when the bread is just perfectly baked, and by means of wires attached to some very delicate machinery, he can in a moment regulate the speed of the oven to the greatest nicety. The bread is now finished, and the reader can imagine how quickly, when we tell him many barrels have been made while we have been noting down these items. But to illustrate it more thoroughly, it requires about ten minutes to roll a barrel of flour off the side-walk, mix it, knead it, roll it, cut it, shape it, bake it, and pack it, and then turn it out as a barrel of crackers. Such is one of the benefits of steam.

After the crackers have arrived at this stage, many would suppose that they were finished; but such is not the case. From the basement the baskets are passed by means of steam-elevators to the third, fourth, and fifth floors, where the contents are spread on the floor the whole length and breadth of the building, to the depth of six or eight inches, presenting a peculiar appearance to the unaccustomed eye, and are there left till thoroughly dry, as without this precaution they would not keep when packed. From these floors men are constantly employed packing and preparing them for transportation. The packing process, simple as it may seem to some, requires considerable practice to be expert at. The men, seated with piles of crackers on either side and the barrel placed horizontally before them, seize and pack with incredible rapidity, in layers, each cracker separately. This house manufactures a large amount of ship biscuit for the use of the British troops and sailors stationed or calling at the British West India Islands. All this bread is packed in bags, being the usual manner of packing in England; but the quality made here is better, and the price lower than it can be obtained for, from that country, hence the trade that has sprung up here. Besides exporting the soldiers' bread, the residents of Barbadoes and other West India Islands highly esteem some of our finer kind of crackers, and a large trade is carried on by the firm in this branch of the business.

At their capacious double store in Warren and Washington streets, as before mentioned, the finer kind of domestic crackers and biscuits are manufactured, but the difference of manufacture simply consists in the mixture of the ingredients, the same kind of machinery and the same kind of oven is employed, while the same never-ceasing activity is displayed; each employee having to be very active to meet the demands of the ever-restless steam horse. It will not be necessary, therefore, to enter into a detail of the premises, but simply to mark the peculiar features, one of which is, that owing to its larger area there is generally stored here a vast amount of flour for consumption, and a quantity of bread to supply customers; but at the present moment, although the flour department is tolerably full, the bread department, owing to the large increased demand, presents simply " a beggarly account of empty barrels" waiting to be filled. In the house on Washington street, in a small room by themselves, are piled up a number of barrels containing what is technically called sweepings; they comprise the broken crackers, cracker dust, and such like, and are sold at cheap rates to farmers for feeding pigs and fowls, and are eagerly bought; thus nothing in this vast establishment is lost, but all is made subservient to man's use.

Such is a very imperfect illustration of the cracker bakery

business, but it may give an idea of how a business, when conducted by *energy, perseverance, system,* and *attention,* may be successful in rising to the front ranks; and as a further proof of the efficacy of these all-important business qualifications, we may mention that during the whole forty years this house has been in business, notwithstanding all the panics and commercial disasters, of which there have been so many in that period, they have always preserved an untarnished credit.

Messrs. E. Treadwell's Sons, with their present facilities, can execute orders or contracts to any amount, either for governments or merchants; and the quality of their manufacture will speak for itself by the reputation it has acquired all over the world.

PETROLEUM.—An important discovery in regard to the practical uses of Petroleum or rock oil now found in such quantities, has been made by Mr. John Lamb, a tanner of Pennsylvania. Since August he has been using the oil in his tannery, as a substitute for fish oil, with most astonishing success. Hides tanned with it have been exhibited to practical leather-dealers from Pittsburgh and Boston, and a quantity sent to the eastern markets, with entire satisfaction. It makes a cleaner and smoother finish than the fish oil, fills up instead of opening the pores of the leather, so as to make it almost water-proof, and gives it the finish of the finest calf-skin. It is also a superior article for mixing blacking, having the quality of cutting the lamp-black. The smell does not remain after the dressing process is completed. The oil is used in the crude state, costing one-third the price of fish oil.

CIGARS, WINES, BRANDIES, &c.

> Oh! grant me, Heaven, a middle state,
> Neither too humble nor too great;
> More than enough for nature's ends,
> With something left to treat my friends.

THOMAS G. LITTLE, 99 LIBERTY STREET, NEW YORK.

This house possesses peculiar facilities for supplying both domestic and imported cigars, and also for cigars made here of the best Havana tobacco. Having agents in Cuba, they can always obtain the best kind of leaf for manufacturing, and also the best cigars in that market. Mr. LITTLE has been over twenty years in the business, and has therefore attained that experience which enables him to purchase to advantage, both as regards quality and price; and, doing a heavy trade, can sell to equal advantage to the buyer.

In the domestic department his facilities are equally as good. His store in Liberty street is five stories high, the whole upper four stories being used for manufacturing, which, when in full blast, gives employment to over two hundred and fifty hands. On the first floor is the warehouse, counting-room, &c. In this warehouse are samples and packages of every description and quality of cigars, while the basement and sub-cellar are filled with the raw material, which, notwithstanding their capacity, are constantly being emptied and replenished.

In connexion with the cigar business, T. G. L. is the sole agent for the Cavalier and Green Seal Champagne, which has attained such a high reputation both in Europe and this country. Connoisseurs want no commendation of this wine. He is also agent for El. Sol. Cognac Brandy, which, although a comparatively recent brand, has yet already attained a strong hold on public favor, and is esteemed by judges most highly for its purity and piquant flavor.

Country merchants visiting this city, and requiring these articles, we recommend visiting 99 Liberty street (west of Broadway), where they can buy on favorable terms, and have the advantage of a large assortment to select from.

HORSES AND CATTLE IN THE WORLD.

An illustrated natural history of the animal kingdom has just been published by S. G. Goodrich. It has 2,400 engravings. It is a highly useful work. Among other information abounding in it, it contains the following, which is an estimate of the number of horses in the world. From this we extract the following:

The general estimate has been eight to eighteen horses in Europe to every hundred inhabitants. Denmark has forty-five horses for every hundred inhabitants, which is more than any European country. Great Britain and Ireland have 2,500,000 horses; France has 3,000,000; Austrian empire, exclusive of Italy, 2,600,000; Russia has 3,500,000; the United States have 5,000,000 horses, which is more than any European country; the horses of the whole world are estimated at 57,420,000. Russia has 22,000,000 cattle; Great Britain and Holland have 8,000,000; Austria has 19,000,000; France 8,000,000; United States of America have 22,000,000. The whole world is estimated to contain 210,000,000. It is supposed that one-third of them are killed annually, so that we have about 280,000,000 pounds, 70,000,000 skins, 140,000,000 horns, 280,000,000 feet annually to be converted into beef, tallow, leather, combs, glue, etc.

PHOTOGRAPHY AND THE FINE ARTS.

> Look here upon this picture, and on this;
> Two simple efforts of our modern art;
> See, what a finish marks this manly brow;
> Each play of feature, every thought itself;
> The sun-like flashing of the rolling eye,
> The lips which almost seem to part and speak,
> To give the world assurance of their life.
>
> SHAKSPEARE.

The immense progress this country has made in mechanical and industrial pursuits during the last decade, has been the admiration of the world, but the progress in the arts and sciences is even more remarkable. To what does our country owe this rapid advancement? Doubtless in the first place to the rapid development of our material wealth; and secondly to the impetus given to foreign travel by the improved, speedy, and safe modes of modern conveyance. A journey across the Atlantic a few years ago was a great feat; now, thanks to steam, it is simply a pleasant little excursion. Our wealthy merchants, knowing of the great treasures of art, the accumulated product of the brains of thousands during many centuries, existing in Europe, with that enlightenment and liberality which characterize them as a class, thought no better use could be made of their money than themselves and families to visit these relics of the past. They went, and they saw; and they came back sadly convinced, that in this respect their country was far behind Europe. But that was no reason it should remain so. Having once seen these beautiful works both ancient and modern, it was natural they should appreciate them, and desire their country to excel in that respect, as much as she does in manufactures. They therefore liberally encouraged all their countrymen and women whose works showed genius or talent, and to this encouragement and appreciation we are indebted for our Churches, Powers, Miss Hosmers, and the other glorious workers in the realms of art. It was to those who are sneeringly alluded to as "our fashionable aristocrats," more than to any others, that we owe our rapid advancement, for although genius is indigenous to all countries, its growth is always slow, when it is not appreciated and encouraged. Miss Flora McFlimsey may perhaps require an immense amount of baggage to transport her habiliments, and then have "nothing to wear," but may not this perpetual longing for something new, be the natural result of her appreciation of the "beautiful!" If our limits permitted, we think we could make a good argument on the subject. But our present purpose is to speak of that branch of the fine arts which was introduced to the world some thirty years ago by M. Daguerre in the form of the daguerreotype. At the time of their introduction they were looked on as wonderful productions, and rose rapidly in public favor. The appreciation they met with, gave an incentive to further improvements, and the original daguerreotype was rapidly followed by the photograph and other improvements which have continued up to the present day, now employing a whole army of artists in producing the most finished specimens of this most beautiful art. Amongst those who have contributed very largely to these improvements, and whose enterprise has placed them in the front ranks of the profession, must be ranked the firm of Messrs. C. D. Fredericks & Co., who have recently opened their new Gallery at 587 Broadway. This gallery is one of the most perfect of the kind in the country; all the modern improvements, and all that science could suggest and experience devise, have been adopted, totally regardless of expense to make it complete, and as it possesses some novel and peculiar features we purpose giving a brief description in this paper.

The building is five stories high, 100 feet deep, and 25 feet frontage. The front entrance takes in the first and second stories to the depth of 12 feet from the sidewalk, and is formed by an arch, 29 feet high, on either side of which are glass cases filled with samples of photography, etc.; a glass-door beyond takes us to the main picture gallery. Here we have a feast for the eye and for the mind. Raised up prominently are life size pictures of persons now figuring in the foremost stages of public life, amongst which are the portraits of Genls. Scott, Morris, and Beauregard, Valentine, the esteemed clerk of the Common Council, the Captain General of Cuba (Serrano) and lady, Mad. La Grange, Joseph Hoxie, and others, too numerous to mention, but all life-like and finished in the highest style of art. Interspersed with these are smaller portraits of well-known characters, as well as some perfect bijoux of landscapes in photography; all these must be seen to be appreciated. But while thus catering to the eye, the animal comforts are not forgotten; the vast gallery is abundantly furnished with sofas, fauteuils, etc., the whole of the furniture and decorations being arranged with an artist's eye, all in perfect harmony. At the extreme end of this gallery is the staircase ascending to the second story; this staircase is one of the features of the establishment, and was designed especially by Messrs. Fredericks to obviate the objections ladies have to ascend an abrupt stairway in a public building, and they have succeeded perfectly in their design. On the second floor are situated five artists' studios, the ladies' dressing-room, and in front the ladies' parlor, both luxuriously furnished; attached to which is a promenade gallery, under cover, where the ladies can view the processions often passing along Broadway, or the ever-restless panorama which is always there. These are designed for their exclusive use, the male bipeds being rigidly excluded from them. At night this floor is lighted by four magnificent chandeliers. Once more ascending, we come to the photograph room, which contains one of the largest skylights in the United States, being twenty-two feet high by twelve feet wide; attached to this are the artists' operating rooms, and in the front part are three studios, occupied by the artists in oil, pastel, and water colors. As much water is required, they have here two large tanks, one holding five hundred and twenty-five gallons, which, when full, weighs four thousand lbs.; and to prevent leakage, these tanks are bolted together, instead of being nailed, as is ordinarily the case. On the next floor is the daguerreotype room, and the artists' manipulating rooms. Every one knows a daguerreotype room, therefore we need not describe it, otherwise than to say it is in perfect keeping with the rest of the establishment —and as the manipulating rooms are always kept dark, we cannot tell much about them, nor do we advise any one to visit for himself, as they always possess a most disagreeable odor of chemicals, which we at least are not desirous of often inhaling. With another slight ascent we get to the negative room, containing twenty thousand negatives; these are the photographs on glass from which the picture you have, dear reader, is taken, and from which an almost indefinite number may be taken. Passing on we come to the printing-room, where the negatives are transferred—a very pretty process— but like the definition once given to metaphysics, "being a thing we don't understand ourselves, we can't describe it to you." Having now got to the top of the building, we descend to take a peep at the basement, and we see two large heaters for heating the building in winter; a pump of very simple construction and action, for pumping the water to the upper floors; sundry tanks, in which the water is kept constantly flowing, used for some of the processes required in the art; a number of empty cases, and other rubbish lying around; and we should not have cared for our visit but that we came at last to a neatly fitted-up room at the rear end, occupied as a store room; in this we found some most beautiful specimens of workmanship, amounting to thousands of dollars, in the shape of cases, frames, lockets, brooches, and other material, from all parts of Europe and America. We have thus partially described some of the prominent features of Messrs. Fredericks' establishment, but we have left one to the last, as being the most peculiar, at the same time the most admirably adapted one of the whole. We allude to the lighting of the gallery at night. In the portico affixed to the ceiling is a reflector (Wyberd's patent) thirty-five inches diameter, having forty-five burners, throwing a brilliant light on everything below, and forming a sun-flower in shape, having a beautiful appearance; in the inside are fourteen branches, pendent from the ceiling, to which is connected a continuous pipe of an oval form, running the whole length of the gallery, containing one hundred and twenty-five jets. These jets throw a brilliant continuous flood of light on the pictures, and present a splendid *coup d'œil;* in fact, we may say it is about the best lighted gallery we have seen.

Of course an establishment of this magnitude requires a considerable number of assistants. Messrs. Fredericks & Co. engage the best of artists, and always have an agreement with them for three years; they have now two in oil, two in pastel, four in India ink, two in water colors, and twelve photographers, daguerreotypists, and printers, besides eleven other assistants. Their business is conducted in the most liberal manner, as they never ask a deposit when an order is left with them, although they have often executed orders that have never been called for. Their enterprise has extended so far, that they have a partner residing in Paris, who keeps them advised of all improvements, and sends them all the novelties. It was this spirit of enterprise that enabled them to be the first to introduce the art, as at present it is, into this country, and we are glad to see that the public have appreciated and recognised their efforts. Those who have never visited Messrs. C. D. Fredericks & Co.'s gallery, at 587 Broadway, we recommend to do so at their earliest convenience, as it is open free till nine o'clock at night, and when they have done it they will thank us for the advice.

AMERICAN GUTTA PERCHA ROOFING CO.

> When fiction rises pleasing to the eye,
> Men will believe, because they love the lie;
> But truth herself, if clouded with a frown,
> Must have some solemn proofs to pass her down.
> —CHURCHILL.

No want has been more generally felt than that of an *Enduring, Elastic, Fire-Proof Roofing*, the cost of which shall be such as to bring it within the reach of all. Shingles of the best quality form a roof that lasts a long time; but the danger from fire renders them unsafe in cities and towns, while the repairs necessitated by the warping and cracking of the shingles are a source of considerable annoyance and expense. Again, shingles require a steep roof, thus increasing the amount of surface, and consequent cost.

Roofs of tin, iron, zinc, or other metal, have failed to answer the demand. They are expensive, and soon become leaky from expansion and contraction, caused by extremes of heat and cold. This separates the joints and cracks the metal surfaces. In process of time, also, these metal roofs rust through. Paint is an outside protection, but needs renewal every year or two; and with even this protection the dampness collected inside the building rusts the metal from beneath.

A large variety of composition roofs have been invented to meet this general want. The principal ingredient in all, or nearly all, of these, is coal tar or asphaltum. Both of these are worse than useless for the purpose. They contain an acid which corrodes the fabrics in contact, and in a short time destroys the roofing material itself. Under the heat of the sun, also, the material melts, a portion of it running off, causing a most disagreeable odor, familiar to all who have used this roofing. The residuum forms into a dry, scaly substance, which is totally incompetent to protect from leakage.

The AMERICAN GUTTA PERCHA ROOFING COMPANY possess the *only patent right* to the use of gutta percha in roofing, and are the only ones whose roofs can be *guaranteed durable and entirely free from leakage.* Several other parties have advertised gutta percha roofing, but without any right to the use of it. Their roofing is coal tar under another name. The roofing manufactured by the above company contains *no coal tar or asphaltum, or other substance of injurious or perishable character.* The Gutta Percha Cement forms a preservative of the highest and most lasting quality, whether in new roofs or applied to metal roofs to protect them from leakage. It is *much cheaper* than metal or tin roofs, and much better. It forms an elastic body which no heat of the sun will melt. It is equally *invaluable for car and steamboat decks.* On cars its elasticity preserves it from the damage liable to other roofs in use. No degree of cold will cause it to crack. From its character it can be applied equally well to flat or steep roofs, according to the taste of those building. It forms a very light roof.

In applying it, a compact saturated cloth is first laid down and tacked. *This cloth is manufactured expressly for the purpose, and is completely water-proof*, being saturated with the Gutta Percha Cement in the manufacture. When the cloth is tacked down two coats of the Gutta Percha Cement are applied to it, and covered with marble dust, which gives a beautiful surface nearly white, as well as making the roof *fire-proof.* This roof will last longer without repair than any other in use.

The agents of the company in New York are Messrs. FORBES & WILLIS, 73 South street. This roofing has been introduced but a comparatively short time in this city, but it is rapidly gaining in popularity, having achieved a decided success in Cincinnati, St. Louis, Chicago, Louisville, Cleveland, &c., where it has been for some years in use, and is pronounced the best roofing material yet invented. It is doubtless destined, from its three great qualities of durability, lightness, and economy, to effect a revolution in the roofing business and supersede all other material.

FORBES & WILLIS, 73 South street, New York, sole agents for the American Gutta-Percha Roofing Company in the State of New York. Cheap, durable, fire-proof Roofing. Leaky roofs repaired with Gutta-Percha Cement.

HOW COFFEE CAME TO BE USED.

It is somewhat singular to trace the manner in which arose the use of the common beverage of coffee, without which few persons, in any half or wholly civilized country in the world now make breakfast. At the time Columbus discovered America, it had never been known or used. It only grew in Arabia and Upper Ethiopia. The discovery of its use as a beverage is ascribed to the superior of a monastery in Arabia, who, desirous of preventing the monks from sleeping at their nocturnal services, made them drink the infusion of coffee, upon the reports of shepherds, who observed that their flocks were more lively after browsing on the fruit of that plant. Its reputation spread through the adjacent countries, and in about two hundred years it had reached Paris. A single plant, brought there in 1714, became the parent stock of all the French coffee plantations in the West Indies. The Dutch introduced it into Java and the East Indies, and the French and Spanish all over South America and the West Indies. The extent of the consumption now can hardly be realized. The United States alone annually consume it at the cost, on its landing, of from fifteen to sixteen millions of dollars.

3*

THE PHOTOGRAPHIC ART.

Can gold calm passion, or 'make reason shine?
Can we dig peace or wisdom from the mine?
Wisdom to gold prefer; for 'tis much less
To make our fortune than our happiness.
                                    YOUNG.

J. GURNEY AND SONS.

In no department of the arts and sciences has the genius of man been more fully developed than in that which pertains to the art of Photography. Twenty or twenty-five years ago, when the art was first introduced, we find the crude and imperfect daguerreotype being looked upon by the wondering public as a great phenomenon, and the production of portraits by aid of the Camera as a complete triumph of genius. And yet, although so few years have elapsed, see the wonderful change! The photograph of to-day is no more to be compared with the daguerreotype of the past than is a gas-light to the sun.

It must not be supposed that the improvements were effected in a moment, or were the work of one individual; on the contrary, they were the work of many, and required much patient persevering labor to attain their present perfection. To Mr. J. Gurney, more than to any other artist, we are indebted for many desirable improvements which he is still continuing. As an evidence of his desire to keep pace with the improvements of the age, he has recently fitted up at great expense the new white marble building, No. 707 Broadway, which for elegance and convenience is unsurpassed in the world, about which we propose giving a few details.

Mr. Gurney's rooms were first opened in 1840, at the time when the art was in its infancy, and were opened previous to any others now in existence; during this period of twenty years he has devoted his entire attention to the perfection of the photographic art, inventing many improvements himself, and advancing large sums of money to others to assist them in demonstrating their supposed discoveries. Indeed, so entirely and enthusiastically was he attached to his art, that he invited and eagerly listened to all suggestions, going to the expense of experimenting on them whether they promised successful results or not, and by this means has often attained vastly different results from what he expected in commencing the experiment.

On entering his present establishment you pass through the beautiful reception room on the first floor, then up one flight of stairs to the exhibition gallery. This is furnished in the most elaborate manner, and adorned with the productions of some of the best American and foreign landscape painters. Here likewise may be seen a large collection of photographs finished in every size and style; among which are those of some of the most eminent persons of the day. Next follow the daguerreotype and photograph operating rooms, both of which are under the personal supervision of Mr. Gurney, and close to these come the artists' studios in oil paintings, and the pastel studios where artists of the first distinction labor for the perfection of art.

The particular styles of pictures Mr. G. is now producing are as follows, viz.:

PHOTOGRAPHS.—From miniature to life-size finished in oil, pastel, water-colors, India ink and Crayon, by a corps of talented artists.

IMPERIAL.—Retouched and plain photographs.

MINIATURES IN OIL.—For beauty, delicacy, and finish, are unequalled.

IVORYTYPES.—This new and beautiful style of portraiture

has all the correctness of a plain photograph, combined with the finish of the most delicate miniature on ivory.

Daguerreotypes—In the usual artistic styles.

Photographic Visiting Cards.—A unique and beautiful article, to which ladies' attention is especially directed.

Old Daguerreotypes of deceased persons can be copied by the photographic process, enlarged to any size, and colored in any style equal to those made from life.

Messrs. J. Gurney and Sons' Gallery, at 707 Broadway, is open (free) daily till nine p.m., where they invite the public to inspect their very large collection of photographs, and we can conceive of no place where a half hour could more pleasantly or profitably be spent.

Precious Metal Production.—The value of the production of precious metals, per annum, in different countries, is as follows: United States, $80,000,000; Great Britain, $100,000,000; Russia, $25,000,000; France, 15,000,000; Austria, $2,500,000; Prussia, $20,000,000; Belgium, $1,0000,000; Spain, $7,500,000; Sweden and Norway, 5,000,000; Saxony, $1,500,000; Italy, $2,500,000; Switzerland, $390,000; Australia itself produces 41,250,000; Mexico and Chili, $45,000,000; the rest of South America, $7,500,000. According to these figures the annual precious metal crop of Europe, America, and Australia, approximates $380,000,000.

M. Lalande, the French astronomer, during the whole time of the Revolution, confined himself to the study of that science. When he found that he had escaped the fury of Robespierre, he jocosely said, "I may thank my stars for it."

A DIRECTORY TO THE PRINCIPAL OBJECTS OF INTEREST IN NEW YORK.

Academy of Design (National), 58 East Thirteenth street.
Aged Indigent Female Society, 130 East Twentieth street.
Almshouse, Blackwell's Island.
American Bible House, occupies the block of ground bounded by the Fourth avenue, Astor place, Third avenue, and Ninth street, and is six stories high, with cellars and vaults.
American Anti-Slavery Society, 138 Nassau street.
American Baptist Home Mission Society, 115 Nassau street.
American Bible Society, Fourth avenue and Astor place.
American Bible Union, 350 Broome.
American Board of Commissioners for Foreign Missions, Bible House, Astor place.
American Congregational Union, 348 Broadway.
American Geographical and Statistical Society, University Building, University place.
American Home Mission Society, Bible House, Astor place.
American Institute, 351 Broadway.
American Missionary Association, 48 Beekman.
American Museum, Broadway, c. Ann street.
American Seaman's Friend Society, 80 Wall.
American Sunday-School Union, 375 Broadway.
American Temperance Union, 149 Nassau.
American Tract Society, 150 Nassau.
American and Foreign Christian Union, 156 Chambers.
American and Foreign Bible Society, 115 Nassau.
Apprentices' Library, 472 Broadway.
Arsenal of the State of New York, Fifth avenue and Sixty-fifth street.
Arsenal (City), Elm, c. White.

Assay Office, 20 Wall.
Astor Library, Lafayette place, n. Broadway.
Baptist Historical Society, 115 Nassau.
Bellevue Hospital occupies a considerable part of the area bounded by Twenty-sixth and Twenty-eighth streets, 1st avenue.
Bloomingdale Insane Asylum, south of Manhattanville, between One Hundred and Fifteenth street and One Hundred and Twentieth street.
Board of Domestic Missions of Dutch Reformed Church, 337 Broadway.
Board of Publications of Dutch Reformed Ch., 337 Broadway.
Brooklyn Athenæum, Atlantic, c. Clinton.
Brooklyn Lyceum, Washington, c. Concord.
Brooklyn Post-office, Fulton, n. City Hall.
Central Education Society, Bible House.
Children's Aid Society, Clinton Hall, Astor place.
City Hall, in the Park.
City Hospital, 323 Broadway, op. Pearl.
City Prison (Tombs), Centre, c. Franklin.
City Sunday-School Society of M. E. Church, 199 Mulberry.
Colonization Society, Bible House, Astor place.
Colored Home, First avenue and Sixty-fourth street.
Colored Orphan Home, Fifth avenue and Forty-second street.
Columbia College, Fourth avenue and Fiftieth street.
Congregational Union, 348 Broadway.
Cooper Institute, Fourth avenue and Eighth street.
Custom House, c. Wall and Nassau streets, extending through to Pine street.
Deaf and Dumb Asylum, Washington Heights, near Fort Washington, $9\frac{3}{4}$ miles from the City Hall, and commanding a splendid view of the Hudson river.
Debtors' Prison, 22 Eldridge.

Eye and Ear Infirmary, Second avenue and Thirteenth street.

Female Missionary Society of M. E. Church, 200 Mulberry.

Five Points House of Industry, numbers 155, 157, and 159 Worth street, a short distance north of the City Hall.

Free Academy of the City of New York, Twenty-third street, c. Lexington avenue.

Gallery of Fine Arts, Second avenue and East Eleventh street.

General Society of Mechanics and Tradesmen, 472 Broadway.

Geographical and Statistical Society, University Building, University place.

Halls of Justice and City Prisons, cover the block of ground bounded by Centre, Leonard, Elm, and Franklin streets—fronting on Centre.

Hall of Records, is situated in the Park, a short distance northeast of the City Hall.

House and School of Industry, 100 West 16th street.

House of Refuge, Randall's Island.

Home for the Friendless, 32 East 30th street.

Institution for the Blind, occupies the whole block between 33d and 34th streets, and Eighth and Ninth avenues.

Irish Emigrant Society, 51 Chambers street.

Ladies' Home Mission of M. E. Church, 200 Mulberry.

Leake and Watts Orphan Asylum, 111th street and Eighth avenue.

Lodging House for Newsboys, 128 Fulton.

Lunatic Asylum, 117th street, n. Tenth avenue.

Lyceum of Natural History, Medical College, 14th street, n. Third avenue.

Lying-in Hospital, 85 Marion.

Magdalen Female Benevolent Society, Tenth avenue and Eighty-eighth street.

Marine Temperance Society of Port of New York, 190 Cherry street.

Mariners' Family Industrial Society, 322 Pearl.
Mechanics' Institute, 20 Fourth avenue.
Mechanics' and Tradesmen's Society, 472 Broadway, and 32 Crosby street.
Merchants' Exchange occupies the entire block of ground between Wall, William, and Hanover streets, and Exchange place.
Methodist Book Concern, 200 Mulberry.
Mercantile Library, Clinton Hall, Astor place.
Missionary Society of M. E. Church, 200 Mulberry.
Nursery for Poor Children, 223 Sixth avenue.
New Courthouse, at the northeast corner of the Park.
New York Hospital, Broadway, occupies most of the block between Worth and Duane streets.
New York Association for Improving the Condition of the Poor, Bible House, Astor place.
New York Bible Society, 7 Beekman.
New York Bible and Common Prayer Book Society, 55 East Thirteenth street.
New York City Temperance Alliance, 114 Grand.
New York City Tract Society, Nassau, c. Spruce.
New York City Sunday-School of M. E. Church, 200 Mulberry street.
New York Historical Society, University Buildings.
New York Marine Bible Society, 80 Wall.
New York Port Society for Promotion of the Gospel among Seamen, 80 Wall.
New York Sunday-School Union, 375 Broadway.
New York Typographical Society, 3 Chambers.
New York University, Wooster street, c. Waverley place.
New York Woman's Hospital, 83 Madison avenue.

New York Young Men's Christian Association, Clinton Hall, Astor place.

New York Orphan Asylum, Bloomingdale and Seventy-first street.

Penitentiary, Blackwell's Island.

Presbyterian Domestic Mission Society, 23 Centre.

Presbyterian Education Society, 23 Centre.

Presbyterian Foreign Mission Society, 23 Centre.

Presbyterian Publication Society, 23 Centre.

Prison Association of New York, 15 Centre.

Protestant Episcopal Domestic Mission Society, Bible House, Astor place.

Protestant Episcopal Foreign Mission Society, Bible House, Astor place.

Protestant Episcopal Sunday-School and Church Book Society, 637 Broadway.

Protestant Episcopal Tract Society, 55 East Thirteenth street.

Protestant Half Orphan Asylum, 142 Sixth avenue.

Public School Society, Grand, c. Elm.

Roman Catholic Half Orphan Asylum, Mott, c. Prince.

Rotunda, near the northeast corner of the Park.

Rutgers Female Institute, 244 Madison.

Sailors' Home, 190 Cherry.

Sailors' Snug Harbor, Office, 115 Wall.

Seventh Day Baptist Mission Society, 9 Spruce.

Seventh Day Baptist Publication Society, 9 Spruce.

Stuyvesant Institute, 659 Broadway.

Surrogate's Office, 3 Hall of Records, and Register's Office, 1 and 2 Hall of Records.

Tract Society of Methodist Episcopal Church, 200 Mulberry.

Trinity Church, Broadway.

Union Theological Seminary, 9 University place.

THE GROVER AND BAKER SEWING MACHINE COMPANY'S ESTABLISHMENT.

> The fame that a man wins himself, is best;
> That he may call his own. Honors put on him
> Make him no more a man than his clothes do,
> Which are as soon ta'en off.
> MIDDLETON.

The Grover and Baker Company is one of the oldest and most successful of the originators and directors of the business. It entered the field at an early day, when sewing machines were almost in their first stages —when their manufacture was more of an experiment than anything else; step by step it has progressed in the development of the trade and the perfecting of its machines; taking advantage of all possible improvements in the make, adaptation, and modification of the machinery, it has enjoyed the exclusive benefits of the inventive genius of one person of the firm (Mr. William O. Grover), by which it has been placed in possession of privileges and patents that have given its machines peculiar and exclusive excellences, until now, we find the company strong in resources, quick in the enterprise of competition, exercising a marked influence on the times by its taste and liberality, and diffusing good results to society, to morals, and to the happiness of our kind.

The building erected by the Company, for its exclusive use, is situated in Broadway (No. 495), in the St. Nicholas Hotel block, between Broome and Spring streets, and on the promenade side of the great thoroughfare. It has a front of twenty-five feet, with a depth of two hundred feet, extending through to Mercer street. In this fine area are comprised some of the most beautiful rooms to be found upon the "street of superb stores."

Thus, in the basement is the *Packing Room*, two hundred feet long by twenty-five feet in width, while the *Repair Shop* extends out beneath the walk and street, giving a fine room twenty-five by twenty-five feet.

The first floor, *Sales Room*, is one hundred and fifty feet long, by twenty-five in width. Back of it is a *Fitting-up Room*, fifty by twenty-five feet, fronting on Mercer street.

The second floor comprises the main *Tuition Room* (called the Ladies' Parlor), one hundred and fifty feet in length by twenty-five in width. Back of this room is the *Ware Room for Cabinets* and tables, fifty by twenty-five feet.

The third floor comprises a room twenty-five by fifty feet, devoted to storage and packages awaiting orders.

These leading rooms are beautifully and tastefully furnished. Walls are in hard finish; floors are carpeted with tapestry, velvet, and Brussels; mirrors adorn the sides; a piano is at hand; sofas are disposed around in a most inviting manner; and a well-chosen library offers its treat to all, while machines of every pattern, size, and style, occupy the floors in long lines and numbers which bewilder the eyes. The whole is lighted by four sky-lights or "wells," three of which are seventeen feet in length, by eight feet four inches in width, oval-shaped. They are guarded by heavily built railing. From the first to the second floor springs a fine flight of stairs. The salesroom is lighted, at night, by seven richly mounted chandeliers, of six burners each. Upon the right side of this room, as you enter, is the counter and goods' shelving, where the purchaser obtains needles, silk, thread, etc., etc.—everything being kept on sale which may be required for the successful working of the machine. Beyond the counter are the desks of the book-keepers, cashier, advertising agent, etc. Machines occupy the left side and centre of the floor, running through the whole length. On the second floor, or Ladies' Parlor, are machines disposed to suit the convenience of the operators. It is in this room that persons buying a machine are taught how to work it successfully. Skilful and obliging lady operators are in attendance, to render all necessary assistance, and an hour or two generally suffices to initiate the most inexperienced into the mysteries of the whole thing—practice, then, only being necessary to make a rapid and good sewer.

When the Sewing Machine was first invented there was a great outery against it—it would ruin the poor seamstress, thousands of tailors, shirt-makers, and others, who get their living by the needle, would be thrown out of employment, and the work would only be imperfectly done. But how different has been the result! Instead of ruining the seamstresses, it has benefited them; instead of throwing out of employment it has engendered more, and by reason of its great power of rapid production it has placed all articles of clothing within the reach of the poorest. In fact, it has proved one of the greatest benefactors of the age.

The Sewing Machine, as originally invented, formed what is known as the *shuttle stitch*. The insecurity, want of strength, and elasticity of this stitch early attracted the attention of Mr. W. O. Grover, who, after long, patient, and persevering labor, patented in 1851 their celebrated *lock-stitch*, which achieved the desired results, combining strength, security, and elasticity of seam. Messrs. Grover and Baker, however, were not satisfied with their first attainment; they still persevered in their researches, and in 1852, '53, and '58, obtained patents for some further improvements. But their crowning glory was the obtaining a patent for the "Noiseless" Machine, which runs with such ease as to do away with the iritating rumble and clicking that had previously rendered the work-room of a large factory a pandemonium of bewildering noise, and the presence of a machine in a private house little else than a nuisance when in operation.

Messrs. Grover and Baker's Machines seem pretty nearly to have reached a perfect point; but should the requirements of the times suggest any new improvements, the ingenuity of the firm, we doubt not, would soon attain them.

The mercurial electric light, now in use in England, is said to be the strongest and purest light in the known world—the nearest approach to sunlight that modern science has yet produced. It is caused by the application of electricity from a voltaic battery to a thin stream of quicksilver, which is heated to a white heat; as impossible to look at with the naked eye, as the sun at noonday.

COAL OILS.

> Thus every object of creation
> Can furnish hints for contemplation;
> And from the most minute and mean
> A virtuous mind can morals glean.
>
> Gay's Fables.

The manufacture of coal oils is comparatively of recent origin in this country, but yet, notwithstanding its youth, there are already some colossal establishments for the manufacture of Petroleum, Kerosene, Paraffine, &c., one of the largest of which we purpose describing in the present paper, believing it to possess features of much interest to the general public.

The establishment we allude to is situated on Newtown Creek, known by the name of the New York Kerosene Oil Company, Messrs. Cozzens & Co. It is about one mile from the Tenth-street Greenpoint ferry, on the Flushing Railroad, which runs through the centre of their works. On the lower side of the railroad are situated the distilling works, and on the upper, the refining, finishing, &c.

On entering the lower side we first encounter a number of queer looking brick structures, which we are told are meerschaums. They are eighteen in number, and are charged with twenty-five tons of coal each; the coal is then subjected to a gradual heat from above—about 700° temperature—which extracts the oil from the coal, forcing it into a condenser, from whence it passes in a crude state, a thick black liquid mass, into the various reservoirs that are sunk all over this part of the factory. In the neighborhood of these meerschaums are the still-houses, containing eighteen stills, into which the crude oil is pumped. In the whole of the works, there are fifty-five stills used for the different refining processes. Having learned so much of the process, we proceed down towards the creek. Here we find a fine wharfage front of seven or eight hundred feet, with schooners and barges loading and unloading. On the east end is situated the coal yard, occupying nearly an acre and a half of ground. Over this is erected a series of scaffolding, composed of very strong timbers, forming three railways, at a height of thirty feet from the ground, on which the coal is hoisted from the boats by means of a steam engine, and then distributed all over this space. The requirements of the factory are about thirty thousand tons of coal a year, and to keep a supply always ready to hand, necessitates the piling up of coal on the wharf; hence the use of this scaffolding and railroad.

From the wharf we retrace our steps till we come to a brick building situated near the railroad, where are six Worthington pumps, worked by steam, employed in pumping the crude oil from the reservoirs on this ground to the reservoirs on the refining ground, to be again pumped into the different receptacles for its thorough purification into kerosene. This process employs seventeen steam pumps. From hence we cross the railroad and enter the finishing ground. Here, in consequence of the increased demand of late years, vast improvements have taken place and are still in progress. We first come upon the coopers' shop, a large, commodious structure, where all the barrels are made and coopered. Next we come to the alkali house, a small building, but important in the manufacture. We then pass on to the purifying house, containing eight agitators. This is the first process of purification through which the crude oil passes. It is here pumped up from the reservoirs by the steam pumps into the agitators, which are large tubs about fifteen feet high by eight feet in diameter, capable of holding three thousand gallons each; in the centre of these is a kind of fan, or screw, worked by steam power. After the oil is pumped in certain chemicals and acids are mixed with it, the steam is then turned on, and the whole mass is kept in a perpetual whirl. We looked into one while it was in this active state, and—smelt kerosene for a week afterwards. The engine that supplies the power required for the whole of the departments on this ground is one hundred horse-power, and is one of the simplest, although the most perfect, ever used in a manufacturing establishment. It has three boilers, and the chimney —one hundred and twenty-five feet high—is a fine specimen of brick-work, and forms a landmark for the surrounding country.

After passing through the first process of refinement it is sent into other stills, where it undergoes a still further process of purification, and is finally deposited, by means of more steam-pumps, in the four receiving tanks, each capable of holding seven thousand gallons, contained in the two receiving houses. From hence it is barrelled for market. This barrelling process, however, is much indebted to the inventive genius of the age for new improvements. By the old process the requirements of the house would take twenty men to do what six or seven can do now. A very ingenious contrivance in the shape of a meter (Worthington's patent), is fastened on to each of the spigots of the finishing tanks, by which means the oil is measured into the barrel as fast as it can run out, never failing to indicate the true measure. This invention the firm has found most useful, not only for home consumption, but in filling the large orders they have for Australia. The oil shipped for Australia, owing to the length of voyage, has to be packed in five-gallon tin cans, two placed in a box, and had they to fill them by the ordinary method, the time consumed in doing it would be three times as long, and the price of the article advanced in equal proportion.

We have thus given a very hasty description of the manufacture of kerosene, but to better understand the extent of this department of labor, we will give some details connected with this one house alone. Their various buildings cover an area of about eight acres, and these buildings are rendered as nearly fire-proof as possible. They have two tanks erected, capable of holding in each ninety thousand gallons of oil, and have five more building of the same capacity, with one capable of holding one hundred and fifty thousand gallons, to provide for all future wants. They can at the present moment turn out twelve thousand gallons of oil per day, and when the tanks before mentioned are finished they will be enabled to keep on hand nearly a million gallons. Two hundred men are constantly employed here, besides others occasionally engaged. The thirty thousand tons of coal used annually employ a large number more in its production and shipment, as does also the shipment of the oil produced, which, taken together, will sum up a very large total of labor employed.

Having thus far only spoken of coal oil or kerosene, our article would be incomplete did we not mention two other articles introduced by this manufacture, one called Paraffine and the other Sludge. The first is the residuum found after the refining process of the oil has been gone through. It is a hard wax-like substance found in particles, which are taken to the paraffine house and there placed between heavy canvas cloths and subjected to a heavy pressure by means of steam machinery, to express any remaining oil and unite the particles in a solid mass. These are sold to candle manufacturers, and produce a candle equally as pure and a light as brilliant as any wax. The second is the residuum of the original crude oil, as we said before, called sludge. This sludge is collected from the tanks, placed in a receptacle used for the purpose, and carried from thence by means of pipes to a large furnace where it is burnt up. This operation does not require any coal for its consumption after the first application of heat, as it possesses the power of producing in a state of fusion the calorie for its own consumption. We cannot help thinking that this is a total waste of the raw material, but as the business is only in its infancy we may hope to see this remedied some day.

In conclusion, we think this manufacture, being now established as one of the necessities of the age, must always progress. The oils are valuable as solvents and lubricators, as well as for photogenic purposes. In the latter use, they give a whiter and more brilliant light than any fixed or fat oil, and are produced at much less cost than oil can be had for. Fish and lard oils are nearly superseded by them, and while they thus prevent the cost of such from rising to any unusual extent in the market, they are themselves controlled by the prices of these oils; and it only requires sufficient attention to be bestowed on its purification, so as to free it from its creasote impurities, to render it one of the most pleasing and brilliant, as well as the safest and most economic sources of light in those situations where gas is not desirable or attainable.

The counting-house of Messrs. Cozzens & Co. is at 89 Water street, New York, where all the general business of the firm is transacted, to which address all orders should be transmitted.

An editor in a country town, who was warmly pressed during a contest to give his vote to a certain candidate, replied that it was impossible, since he had already promised to vote for the other. "Oh," said the candidate, "in election matters, promises, you know, go for nothing." "If that is the case," rejoined the elector, "I promise you my vote at once."

POPULATION OF THE UNITED STATES.

The Superintendent of the Census has prepared the following table of the census of the several States and Territories, the slave population, and the number of Representatives to which each State is entitled:

	Free Population.	Slave Population.	37th Congress Representatives.
Maine...................	619,958	———	5
New Hampshire..........	326,072	———	3
Vermont................	315,827	———	3
Massachusetts...........	1,231,494	———	10
Rhode Island............	174,621	———	1
Connecticut.............	460,670	———	4
New York...............	3,851,563	———	30
Pennsylvania............	2,916,018	———	23
New Jersey.............	676,084	———	5
Delaware...............	110,548	1,805	1
Maryland...............	646,183	85,382	5
Virginia................	1,097,373	495,826	11
North Carolina..........	679,965	328,877	7
South Carolina..........	308,186	407,185	4
Georgia................	615,336	467,461	7
Florida................	84,885	63,809	1
Alabama...............	520,444	435,473	6
Mississippi.............	407,051	479,607	5
Louisiana..............	354,245	312,186	4
Arkansas...............	331,710	109,065	3
Texas..................	415,999	184,956	4
Tennessee..............	859,528	287,112	8
Kentucky...............	820,077	225,490	8
Ohio...................	2,377,917	———	19
Indiana................	1,350,802	———	11
Illinois.................	1,691,238	———	13
Missouri...............	1,085,599	115,610	9
Michigan...............	734,291	———	6
Wisconsin..............	768,485	———	6
Iowa...................	682,002	———	5
Minnesota..............	172,793	———	1
Oregon	52,566	———	1
California..............	384,770	———	3
Kansas.................	143,645	———	1
Total of States....	27,385,439	3,999,853	233

POPULATION OF THE TERRITORIES.

Nebraska	28,893
New Mexico	93,024
Utah	50,000
Dakotah	4,839
Washington	11,624
District of Columbia	75,321
Total of Territories	263,701

RECAPITULATION.

Free population in all States and Territories in United States	27,649,140
Slave population	3,999,853
Total population	31,648,993

DISCOVERIES BY THE MICROSCOPE.

Leuwenhoeck tells us of animated insects seen with the microscope, of which twenty-seven millions would only be equal to a mite. Insects of various kinds are observable in the cavities of a common grain of sand. Mould is a forest of beautiful trees, with the branches, leaves, flowers, and fruit fully discernible. Butterflies are fully feathered. Hairs are hollow tubes. The surface of our bodies is covered with scales like a fish; a single grain of sand would cover 150 of these scales, and a single scale covers 500 pores. Yet through these narrow openings the sweat exudes like water through a sieve. How minute then must be its particles! The mite makes 500 steps in a second. Each drop of stagnant water contains a world of animated beings, swimming with as much liberty as whales in the sea. Each leaf has a colony of insects grazing on it like oxen in a meadow.

POPULATION OF THE EARTH.

The Directors of the Statistical Bureau of Berlin furnish the following curious statement: The population of the whole earth is estimated to be 1,288,000,000, viz. Europe, 272,000,000; Asia, 755,000,000; Africa, 200,000,000; America, 50,000,000; and Australia, 2,000,000. The population of Europe is thus subdivided: Russia contains 62,000,000; the Austrian States, 36,398,620; France, 36,039,364; Great Britain and Ireland, 27,488,853; Prussia, 17,089,407; Turkey, 18,740,000; Spain, 17,518,000; the Two Sicilies, 8,616,922; Sweden and Norway, 5,072,082; Sardinia, 4,976,034; Belgium, 4,607,066; Bavaria, 4,547,239; the Netherlands, 3,486,016; Portugal, 3,471,199; the Papal States, 3,000,000; Switzerland, 2,494,500; Denmark, 2,468,648. In Asia, the Chinese empire contains 400,000,000; the East Indies, 171,000,000; the Indian Archipelago, 90,000,000; Japan, 35,000,000; Hindostan and Asiatic Turkey, each 15,000,000. In America, the United States are computed to contain 23,191,876; Brazil, 7,677,800; Mexico, 7,661,520. In the several nations of the earth there are 335,000,000 of Christians, of whom 180,000,000 are Catholics, 80,000,000 Protestants, and 76,000,000 followers of the Greek Church. The number of Jews amounts to 5,000,000; of these, 2,890,750 are in Europe, viz. 1,250,000 in European Russia; 853,304 in Austria; 234,248 in Prussia; 192,107 in other parts of Germany; 62,470 in the Netherlands; 33,953 in Italy; 73,995 in France; 35,000 in Great Britain; 70,000 in Turkey. The followers of Asiatic religions are estimated at 600,000,000; Mohammedans at 160,000,000; and Heathens (the Gentiles proper) at 200,000,000.

In the tongue of the right whale there are from 300 to 800 gallons of oil!

SOMETHING ABOUT DRY GOODS.

> Of all the passions that possess mankind,
> The love of novelty rules most the mind;
> In search of this, from realm to realm we roam,
> Our fleets come fraught with every folly home.
>
> FOOTE.

At what time the trade in dry goods became a separate branch of merchandise, it is difficult to determine. The Romans had separate mechanical and mercantile fraternities, from which the modern guilds traceable to the tenth century have descended. But the dry goods trade as at present organized is of quite modern origin, neither the importer, commission merchant, jobber, nor retailer, having until the last few years confined himself exclusively to the sale of dry goods. This may be easily accounted for by considering the immense increase during the last few years in the consumption of these goods, which has at the present moment rendered this trade, considered as a branch of commerce, one of the most important of any now existing in the country. It controls a greater amount of capital, employs a larger number of persons, and distributes a greater value of commodities than any other branch of mercantile pursuit. Take for example the marble palaces of the dry goods merchants of New York, and then go through the cities, towns, and villages in the length and breadth of the country, and you will find the list of dry goods merchants far larger than that of any others engaged in the sale of any other specialty of merchandise. In the smaller towns and villages the name of "merchant" is always associated with one who, whatever else he may sell, is sure to have a good assortment of dry goods. There are certainly "merchant princes" among those engaged in other branches of business, but in capacity, energy, and aggregate wealth, the dealers in dry goods as a class are emphatically the *merchants* of our day and country.

An assortment of dry goods may be classed under five principal headings, viz. *woollens, cottons, silks, linens, and miscellaneous*, but these embrace an almost exhaustless variety of articles, and it requires a long apprenticeship in each branch to attain anything like an accurate judgment to meet the requirements of the public as to quality and style, and in this respect is much more difficult to acquire than any other mercantile or mechanical pursuit.

To enable our readers more thoroughly to understand this, we will give them the benefit of our experience on a recent visit paid to one of the largest dry goods merchants of New York. We allude to the firm of C. W. & J. T. Moore & Co., at Nos. 326, 328, and 630 Broadway. The senior partner of this house has been in the business forty years, but the firm under its present title was not formed until 1836, and is now composed of the following members:—Chauncey W. Moore, Jno. T. Moore, Wm. M. Robbins, Emmor K. Haight, Joseph N. Ely, Chauncey W. Brown, Joseph B. Lockwood, and Wm. R. Dean.

They are importers and jobbers of foreign and domestic silks, cloths, vestings, dress goods, prints, hosiery, linens, white goods, every description of American heavy staple goods, and last, although not least, that "olla podrida" known by the title of Yankee notions. The house they occupy is on the site of the old Broadway Theatre, built and owned by Judge Whiting, five stories in height, of white marble, in the purest style of Norman architecture. It has a frontage of seventy-five feet on Broadway, extending backwards one hundred and seventy-five feet, and then at right angles in the form of a T spreading to Worth street with a frontage of seventy-five feet, running from the main store fifty feet, while the extension to Pearl street is seventy-five feet, with a frontage of twenty-five. The whole space embraced in this immense area is eighteen thousand seven hundred and fifty feet. But this detail of the measurement fails to give any idea of the splendid "coup d'œil" presented of the interior of the store as viewed from the rear of the main building, showed most strongly by the powerful vertical light of the immense skylight. Looking towards Broadway between two rows of Corinthian iron pillars supporting the ceiling, forty-three in all, and said to be the largest ever used for the purpose, we see a most tempting display of goods. There are the tasty dainty fabrics of muslin; the innumerable variety of dress goods, formed of every conceivable material, derived from all parts of the world; the inimitable silks, the products of the French looms; the solid, durable articles of England; the cheap and useful goods of Germany, and the thousand and one varieties of American manufacture in dry goods. Turning our eyes towards Worth street we see still more goods, and on the north side, commanding a view of the whole store, a line of busy clerks inclosed in a glass case, where all the records of the transactions of the house are kept. This is the counting house; beyond we have several other partitions, which are the private offices of the members of the firm, while at the extreme end is a luxuriously fitted up parlor, furnished with the daily papers, and every convenience for writing, for the use of the customers of the house. Turning our eyes once again in the opposite direction towards Pearl street, we come upon the Yankee notion department; but we can't describe them—Yankee notions can't be described—let the reader imagine every article he has any idea of, and he will be a long way off from the true conception of the variety of Yankee notions. They must be seen to be imagined. In this wing there is also a very commodiously fitted up room for the use of the employés of the house for reading or writing during their leisure hours. We have thus briefly and imperfectly described the first floor of this establishment, but our impression on entering was that it would be appreciated as a perfect paradise by the Misses Flora McFlimsy and friends, could they only gain access to it, but they are rigidly excluded. Facing each entrance is a notice, *no goods sold at retail.* We think this a piece of cruelty on the part of Messrs. Moore & Co., deserving the severest reprehension, which should be immediately attended to by "the woman's rights convention," who might pass a series of resolutions condemnatory of such cruelty.

Having *done* the first floor, we will now descend to the basement. Under the sidewalk, which is lighted by means of illuminated tiles, and also on the Broadway front of the building, is the white and domestic goods department, whilst in the rear, extending from Pearl to Worth street, two hundred feet in length, are the packing rooms. Here all goods are received, charged, packed, and shipped, and this room is a scene of constant activity, the admirable system enforced in the house enabling the clerks to get through an amount of work which would appear incredible to the uninitiated. From the basement we descend to the sub-cellar, which is used for the storage of whole packages, and is capable of containing many thousands. Under the sidewalk in Worth street are the boilers employed for heating the whole of the building, and for propelling the engines employed in elevating. The whole three floors are lighted by gas, of which there are employed three hundred burners. The fixtures on the first floor are of peculiar beauty, harmonizing with the general architecture of the building, and when the whole forty chandeliers on that floor are in use, with their one hundred and sixty jets, they form a perfect blaze of light.

4*

Our friends in the country may from this hasty sketch gather a partial idea of the magnitude of this trade, and should they visit this city they can gain a better knowledge by inspecting for themselves. We can insure them a courteous welcome by Messrs. Moore & Co., from whom we received every information on the subject their experience commanded.

SIXPENCE A DAY.—There is now an old man in an almshouse, in Bristol, England, who states that for sixty years he spent sixpence a day in drink, but was never intoxicated. A gentleman who heard this statement, was somewhat curious to ascertain how much this sixpence a day, put by every year, at 5 per cent., compound interest, would amount to in sixty years. Taking out his pencil, he began to calculate—putting down the first year's savings (365 sixpences) £9 2s. 6d., he added the interest, 9s. 1½d., and thus went on, year by year, until he found, that in the sixtieth year the sixpence a day reached the startling sum of £3,225 16s. 8d. Judge of the old man's surprise when told, that had he saved his sixpence a day, and allowed it to accumulate at compound interest, he might now have been worth the above noble sum; so that, instead of taking refuge in an almshouse, he might have comforted himself with a house of his own, costing £700, and fifty acres of land, worth £50 an acre, and have left the same as a legacy among his children and grandchildren.

LAW POINT.—What is the difference between an attempted homicide and a hog butchery? One is an assault with intent to kill, and the other is a kill with intent to salt.

PIANO-FORTES.

There's music in the sighing of a reed;
There's music in the gushing of a rill;
There's music in all things if men had ears;
Their earth is but the echo of the spheres.

BYRON.

In no one branch of the industrial arts has greater improvement been made, or more demand created, than in the article of piano-fortes. This is a gratifying evidence that while our country has been increasing enormously in wealth, we have still the time and the inclination to study the fine arts; that, however much the American may love the "almighty dollar," his love is not exclusively confined to that alone.

The manufacture of piano-fortes in New York city has within the last five years nearly doubled itself, there being at the present moment a capital of about $3,000,000 employed in it, while in other parts of the country the increase has been in a corresponding ratio, and we see no appearance of any diminution of demand, but on the contrary new establishments are constantly springing up.

One of the most celebrated establishments in New York for the manufacture and sale of piano-fortes is that of Messrs. Lighte & Bradburys, now reputed to be one of the largest, wealthiest, and most reliable in the country. The origin of this house affords a striking example of the results which inevitably flow from a patient, persevering, and upright course in business. Over thirty years since, Mr. Ferdinand Lighte, whose name now heads the firm, with no other reliance than his own mechanical ability, commenced business with one single piano-forte, which he made entirely, in all its branches, with his own hands. The construction of this instrument, in all its details, imparted to

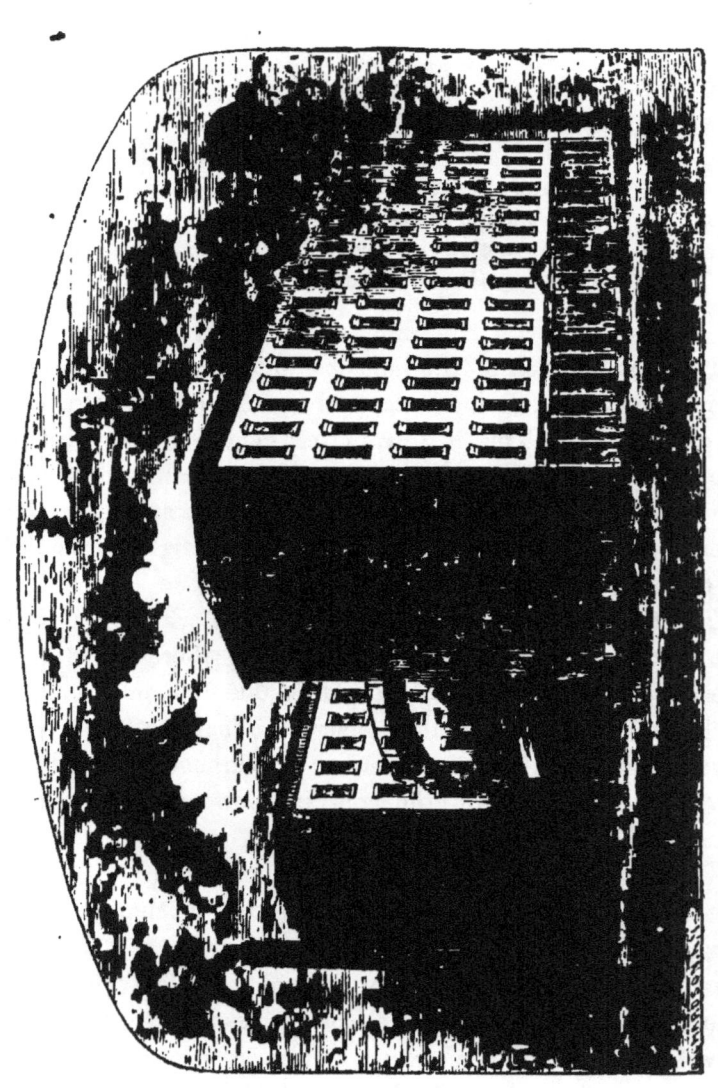

Mr. Lighte a knowledge of all that was necessary to constitute a piano perfect and entire, in every particular. The thought and attention thus given to his early efforts, have since been closely followed up, and by a continued course of patience, energy, and ability, in which he has been ably assisted by all the members of the firm, a confidence has been established in favor of Lighte & Bradburys' manufactures which is equalled by none. Mr. Lighte's experience of thirty years enables him to give his personal inspection to the minutiæ of each instrument, during its whole course of construction, without which no instrument is allowed to leave the establishment, and warrants to the purchaser the possession of every new and valuable improvement in the piano-forte, while the well-earned and worldwide musical reputation of the Messrs. Bradbury is a sufficient guarantee of their superior excellence. The superiority of their instruments is sufficiently guaranteed by the highest order of testimonials in the musical profession—such as Thalberg, Dr. Mason, Strakosch, Timm, Gottschalk, and numerous others. Their manufacturing facilities are not excelled, if equalled, by any in this country. They are producing upwards of twenty-five instruments per week, employing a force of two hundred and fifty men, and a powerful steam engine, which drives some twenty different machines for forwarding the work in an exact and more perfect manner than it can be done by hand, while a large number of hands are employed temporarily, such as workers in pearl, and artists engaged in decorating to suit the peculiar tastes of the fastidious. The materials from which the instruments are made, are seasoned in drying rooms especially suited to the purpose, without which necessary precaution no instrument can successfully withstand the variableness of our climate. It may be proper to remark here that the same care and attention are bestowed upon the plain and lower-priced instruments as upon the more costly ones. The *mechanique*, or action, is made in so perfect a manner that the most delicate expressions in music can be effectively accomplished, and the most powerful interpretations of modern compositions can be rendered without laborious effort to the performer. The many improvements they have introduced in the *modus operandi* of their manufactory, enable the proprietors to defy competition in any specialty of their business.

Wherever their instruments are known, they have a commanding reputation, whether in regard to the excellence of the materials used, the perfection of their mechanism, their superficial embellishments, or their combined power, sweetness, and flexibility of tone. It is proper to remark, that parties at a distance ordering from this house, may rest assured that they will be dealt with as liberally and fairly as if personally present.

Among the many improvements in the piano-forte made by this firm, the patent insulated iron frame takes the first position of any modern invention. The insulators placed between the iron frame and wooden portion of the piano-forte prevent the tinny or metallic quality of tone so justly complained of in the ordinary use of the iron frame, and give freedom to the vibratory portions of the instrument, thereby insuring a durability hitherto unattained, while the singing quality, power, and richness of tone are greatly enhanced. Thus it is appreciated by the most eminent musicians as the *greatest improvement of the age;* and so confident are the manufacturers of its superiority, that they warrant these instruments without limit as to time.

The large capital employed by this firm, and the perfect system with which every detail of the manufacturing department is attended, insure to the purchaser of a Lighte & Bradburys' patent insulated full iron frame piano-forte the best and cheapest instrument manufactured in this country or Europe.

Strangers visiting New York should not neglect the opportunity of visiting the beautiful and spacious warerooms of the firm, 421 Broome street, which are at all times filled with a large and varied assortment of pianos.

NEW DESTRUCTIVE AGENT IN WAR.—Chloride of nitrogen has long been known to chemists as the most terrible detonating compound in existence, so much so that it was considered dangerous to experiment with particles larger than a grain. Mr. Baggs, an English chemist, who has discovered a method for manufacturing it in large quantities, with perfect safety, assures the English government, that one cask of it would, if conveyed into the midst of the largest city, instantly destroy it. It ignites by contact with oil, and a slow match may be placed in a cask of the explosive compound in the shape of a capsule, which the oil would dissolve by the time the operator had escaped to a safe distance.

The Stock Exchange is one of the most remarkable features of London wealth. The government securities alone, and which constitute the national debt, amount to $4,500,000,000; the railway stocks to $1,500,000,000; those of the Bank of England to $150,000,000; to other banks to $350,000,000; employed in discounting, $380,000,000; and besides this, there are shares in canals, foreign lands, &c., to an almost unlimited amount. The stock market is very susceptible of being influenced by political events. The day that it was rumored that Russia and France had formed an alliance, bonds, &c., depreciated $250,000,000, and seventy firms suspended.

THE OIL TRADE.

> She comes majestic with swelling sails,
> The gallant bark; along her watery way
> Homeward she drives before the favoring gales,
> Now flirting at their length the streamers play.
> SOUTHEY.

Many reliable and interesting facts might be adduced to illustrate the value of this highly important and indispensable branch of trade, but want of space precludes the possibility of our giving anything more than a mere summary of statistics and events. The United States tonnage employed in the whale fishery, in the year 1817, was 4,871 tons. It has since then increased, until in 1859 the aggregate was 198,593 tons. The whole number of vessels then employed in the whale fishery, from ports in the United States, is 560 ships and barks, 19 brigs, 45 schooners, including 195,115 tons against 587 ships and barks, 18 brigs, and 49 schooners, including 203,148 tons in the previous year. The importations of sperm oil, during the year 1858, in barrels, were 81,941; whale 182,223, and 1,540,600 pounds of whalebone.

The foreign whale and other fish oils, imported in 1857-8 amounted in value to $18,470.

The importations of sperm oil, in 1858, amounted in all to 81,941 barrels, and of whale oil, to 182,223 barrels.

EXPORTS OF OIL.

	SPERM OIL. Bbls.	WHALE OIL. Bbls.
In 1856	20,052	971
" 1857	37,231	17,407
" 1858	33,336	19,503

The stock of sperm oil in the United States, on the 1st of January, 1859, amounted to 17,176 barrels; that of whale oil to 83,375 barrels. The vessels engaged in the whale fishery are owned in the following states:

States.	Ships and Barks.	Brigs.	Schrs.	Tonnage.
Massachusetts	465	14	32	159,303
Connecticut	54	3	11	22,756
New York	24	2	2	9,219
Rhode Island	13	—	—	5,837
Total	561	19	45	195,115

Of this number, New Bedford alone employs 316 ships and barks. In this beautiful and thriving city, the oil trade is carried on upon an extensive scale. One of the largest and most extensive establishments here, is that of the well-known firm of Messrs. HASTINGS & Co. The location which they have selected is, in all respects, the most desirable in that vicinity, having a fine wharf 400 feet long, which takes in an entire street on each side thereof. Of the large tract of land which they have appropriated to the purpose of their business, not less than three acres are inclosed. This inclosure comprises numerous departments, the most prominent of which is the manufacturing department. The oil which is purchased in its crude state by the cargo, is first conveyed to the works, where it is pumped into immense vats, for the purpose of bleaching, which process is accomplished by means of alkalies. After undergoing the bleaching process, it is then converted into what is known as winter oil. After being conveyed to vats above by means of stationary pumps, it is run thence into the freezing vaults, or ice-house, where it is placed in tanks. The ice-house has a capacity for freezing 1,000 barrels at a time, which is used only during the warm season of the year. The next process is that of running off into strainers, and thence into barrels and casks for market. In the upper portion of the works are numerous tanks, and immense vats capable of containing from 800 to 1,000 barrels. Connected with the establishment, likewise, is a coopering department, and commodious sheds for the storage of stock; one of these sheds is capable of containing, and is usually filled with 25,000 barrels of oil. The establishment throughout is supplied with the best improved machinery, and is unquestionably one of the most important and complete of its kind in the country. This firm was organized in 1846, and comprises the names of Messrs. WAITSTILL, GEORGE, and JOHN HASTINGS, all of whom have been practically educated to their business, and are familiar with it in all its details. The operations of this house extend to all sections of the Union, and their superior manufactures of oils have obtained a celebrity unequalled by that of any other house.

HASTINGS & CO.,

MANUFACTURERS OF

OIL AND CANDLES,

AND DEALERS IN

CURRIERS' OIL,

154 FRONT ST., cor. of Maiden Lane,

NEW YORK.

WAITSTILL HASTINGS, New York
GEORGE HASTINGS, "
JOHN HASTINGS, New Bedford.

Manufactory at NEW BEDFORD.

MILLINERY GOODS.

As lamps burn silent with unconscious light,
So modest ease in beauty shines most bright;
Unaiming charms with rays resistless fall,
And she who means no mischief, does it all.
         AARON HILL.

In New York City alone, there is a capital employed of three millions and a half of dollars in the business of making ladies' hats and caps with the adjuncts included under the head of millinery. This capital is employed by about 500 different establishments; these employ over 8,000 women and girls in their workrooms, besides giving a livelihood to about 1,000 women who do their work at home. It will be a fair calculation to consider, that these women each employ two girls, many more and some less, but the average will be about that.

Thus, we have in the aggregate, 11,000 persons employed in this trade, but this does not represent the number supported by it. Many of the women thus employed have children, some have sick brothers, sisters, and husbands, others old parents, whose only support they are; we may, therefore, safely assume, that from these causes at least 1,500 more may be added to the list, making a total of 12,500 persons supported by this one business.

We recently inspected the extensive millinery establishment of Mr. R. M. MITCHILL, successor to R. T. WILDE & Co., occupying the whole of the upper floors of No. 251 Broadway. Independent of its character as a business house, it possesses attractions which render it well worthy of a visit from strangers.

The large and magnificent stock of goods contained there, is characterized by beauty, novelty, and originality of design, and exhibits, in an eminent degree, the skill and genius of the artists engaged in their production. In the various departments of manufacture, such as the feather making, artificial flower making, bonnet frame making, bonnet finishing, trimming, &c., &c., there are, in the season, over 500 hands employed, mostly in the house, which then presents a scene of life and animation seldom witnessed; we would describe it, but fear our pen would fail to do justice to the scene. Besides this business, Mr. Mitchill is well known throughout the country as an extensive dealer in millinery goods, being largely engaged in the manufacture and importation of straw goods in every variety, silk, velvet, and fancy bonnets, French flowers, feathers, ruches, &c. Merchants from the country, visiting New York to make purchases, will be amply repaid by visiting his establishment and devoting a few hours to an examination of the various departments. No other establishment in New York, in the same business, presents a greater variety or a better assortment of goods; and such are the facilities of the house, that they are enabled to offer unusual inducements to purchasers, both as regards economy in price, elegance of design, and quality of both material and workmanship. Many years' experience in the business has enabled Mr. Mitchill to thoroughly understand the wants of the trade for the various seasons, and the women employed in the millinery department are selected for their skill and taste in meeting the public requirements. That the public and merchants dealing with him have fully appreciated these qualities, his present prosperous business will satisfy all who pay a visit to his store at 251 Broadway, corner of Murray street.

A piano affords a young lady a good chance to show her fingering and her finger-ring.

SILVER WARE.

> Gold is the strength, the sinews of the world,
> The health, the soul, the beauty most divine;
> A mask of gold hides all deformities;
> Gold is heaven's physic, life's restorative.
>
> DECKER.

Silver, the possession of which forms one of the incentives to the pursuit and acquisition of wealth, is obtained principally from Mexico and Peru. The silver mines of Mexico and Peru far exceed in value the whole of the European and Asiatic mines; for we are told by Humboldt, that these mines, in the space of three centuries, afforded 316,023,883 pounds troy of pure silver; and he remarks that this quantity would form a solid globe of silver, 91,206 English feet in diameter. Mr. Helms is of opinion that the Andes, if properly examined, would afford silver enough to overturn our present commercial system, by making silver as common as copper. Silver has also been obtained from some of the lead mines of Great Britain. Bishop Watson, in his "Chemical Essays," notices the silver which was produced from the lead mines in Cardiganshire. Sir Hugh Middleton is said to have cleared two thousand pounds sterling a month, and that this enabled him to undertake the great work of bringing the New River from Ware to London.

Some conception of the amount of silver consumed in the United States may be inferred from the fact that in the year 1858 its importation amounted to $689,533 for the port of New York. Other ports, $6,616,016. Total, United States, $7,305,549.

German Silver (improperly so called) is nothing more than the white copper long known in China, and does not contain a particle of silver; it is only an alloy of copper, metal, and nickel. Amalgam of silver is sometimes used for plating. It may be important to state, in this connexion, for the benefit of those who are in the habit of using plated goods and pure silver ware, that coal gas is highly injurious to them, on account of the sulphuretted hydrogen which they contain.

A large portion of silver is annually diverted from the purposes of coin to those of ornament and luxury. The manufacture of sterling silver ware has of late years grown to a considerable extent, and has now become an important branch of trade. Among the oldest and most reliable houses engaged in this branch of business, may be classed the well-known firm of GALE & WILLIS, whose place of business is located at 447 Broome street, near Broadway. Their beautiful establishment is not only a source of profit to themselves, but of immense benefit to the community; for the unerring principle and vast scale on which their business is conducted, has made it one of the most popular in New York. The manufacture of sterling silver is an important feature of the establishment, and the superb full sets of plate they are constantly furnishing throughout the country, are an evidence of their great superiority. The rich and elegant goods, as they are displayed in the show cases, must be seen to be appreciated. There is one fact, however, which we may notice, and that is, that the patterns and styles of goods differ materially from those to be seen at any other establishment. Some new and attractive feature is constantly produced, either in the shape of some exquisite specimen of the fine arts, or in the form of some article possessing rare value and beauty, such, for instance, as costly and magnificent waiters, epergnes, and services of plate of rare and novel designs.

It may be proper to remark here that the goods of this house are manufactured upon the premises, under the immediate supervision of the proprietors; for which purpose they have a large and well-ordered factory, in which is employed a force of from seventy to eighty skilful artisans, who; with the aid of the most valuable and latest improved machinery, are constantly producing articles which, for beauty and superiority of workmanship, cannot be equalled. The variety of articles manufactured is too numerous to mention, but it is sufficient to state the stock of Messrs. GALE & WILLIS comprises every article usually to be found in establishments of this kind. The house also sells plated ware of foreign and domestic manufacture, and gives special attention to the getting up of prizes for State and county agricultural fairs.

BITUMENIZED PAPER PIPES.—M. Taloureau, of Paris, has devised a method of hardening paper under the influence of hydraulic pressure, by means of an admixture of bitumen, so that it may actually be substituted for iron. Experiments to test the strength of these pipes have been conducted under the great clock tower at the Houses of Parliament in London. Two of the pipes, of five-inch bore and half an inch thick, were subjected to hydraulic power, and they are said to have sustained, without breaking or bursting, a pressure of 220 pounds to the square inch, which is equivalent to 500 feet head of water. The cost of the pipe is said to be one-half that of iron. The committee reported that "the material, possessed all the tenacity of iron with one-half its specific gravity, and double the strength of stone-ware tubes, without, moreover, being liable to breakage as in the case of the other material, which often causes a loss to the contractor of some 20 to 25 per cent. on the supply." Besides the incalculable utility of this discovery, it surpasses the recently-invented paper bricks, or the paper cannon lined with copper which the Chinese are said to have employed for years.

HOTELS IN NEW YORK.

Astor House, Broadway, bet. Barclay and Vesey streets.
Bancroft House, 904 Broadway.
Barclay Street House, West, corner Barclay.
Bixby's Hotel, 1 Park Place.
Bond Street House, 665 Broadway.
Bowery Hotel, 395 Bowery.
Brevoort House, 5th Avenue, corner Clinton Place.
Brandreth House, Broadway, bet. Canal and Lispenard.
Bull's Head, 296 and 298 3d Avenue.
Clarendon, 4th Avenue, corner East 18th street.
Clermont, 12 College Place.
Commercial, 73 Cortlandt street.
Dey Street House, 54 and 56 Dey street.
Earle's, 17 and 19 Park Row.
Eastern Pearl, 309 Pearl street.
Everett House, Union Square, corner 4th Avenue.
Farmers', 247 Washington street.
French's, City Hall Square, cor. Frankfort street.
Girard House, West Broadway, cor. Chambers.
Gramercy House, 908 Broadway, corner 20th street.
Gramercy Park House, East 20th st., near 3d Avenue.
Howard House, 176 Broadway.
Hungerford, 168 Duane street.
International, Broadway, corner Franklin.
Lafarge, Broadway, near Amity.
Lovejoy's, 31 Park Row, corner Beekman street.
Manhattan, 5, 7, 9, Murray street.
Merchants', 37, 39, 41, Cortlandt street.
Metropolitan, Broadway, corner Prince street.
National, 2 and 5 Cortlandt street.

New York, 723 Broadway.
Northern, 79 Cortlandt street.
Pacific, 172 Greenwich street.
Prescott, Broadway, corner Spring street.
Revere, 1085 Broadway.
Smithsonian, 604 Broadway.
St. Denis, Broadway, corner West 11th street.
St. Germains, corner Broadway, 5th Ave. and 22d st.
St. Nicholas, 515 Broadway.
Tammany, 166 Nassau, corner Frankfort street.
United States, 200 Water street.
Union Place, 14th street, corner Broadway.
Waverley, 697 Broadway.
Western, 9, 11, 13 Cortlandt street.

The crown of England is valuable enough to found half a dozen moderate colleges. The twenty diamonds round the circle are worth $150,000; two large centre diamonds, $20,000; fifty-four smaller diamonds in the angle, $270,000; four crosses, each composed of twenty-five diamonds, $60,000; four large diamonds, on the top of the crosses, $20,000; twelve large diamonds, in the *fleur-de-lis*, $50,000; eighteen small ones, in the same, $10,000; pearls and diamonds, in the arches and crosses, $50,000; also one hundred and forty-six small ones, $25,000; twenty-six diamonds, in the upper cross, $150,000; two circles of pearls, about the rim, $15,000; value of precious stones, exclusive of metal, $820,000.

" I shall be indebted to you for life," as the man said to his creditors when he ran away to Australia.

SEWING-MACHINES.

> Learning is an addition beyond
> Nobility or birth: honor of blood
> Without the ornament of knowledge, is
> A glorious ignorance.
>   Shirley.

The Sewing-Machine is no longer an experiment to be tried, but a success achieved, with benefits far exceeding the most sanguine anticipations. The steam-engine, and the magnetic telegraph have not proved more beneficent than this, in its peculiar department. It is one of the greatest triumphs the American people have achieved in the mechanical arts. So fully has this invention commended itself to public favor, that it is now considered indispensable in every branch of industry requiring sewing. Its introduction marks an era in the history of woman. Not only are the wants of the housekeeper met, but the sewing-machine is found a necessity for the seamstress, dressmaker, tailor, manufacturers of shirts, collars, cloaks, mantillas, clothing, hats, caps, corsets, ladies' gaiters, linen and silk goods, umbrellas, parasols, boots, shoes, harness, bags, upholstery, etc. Some of these branches of business have increased to gigantic proportions. It is not unusual to find from 100 to 400 sewing-machines used in a single manufactory. An establishment in New Haven, Ct., employs upwards of 400 Wheeler & Wilson machines in the manufacture of shirts. In and about Troy 3000 of these machines are used in the same business. Mothers support families thereby, and young women become capitalists. It is not unusual to find the owner of a sewing-machine earning from $50 to $100 per month.

Contrary to predictions, the needlewomen have been greatly benefited by the introduction of the machine. New branches

of needlework have been introduced, and the old ones greatly
extended, resulting to the operator in better remuneration and
lighter and more healthful toil. Indeed, the hygienic importance of the sewing-machine is not less than its commercial.
The unhealthful nature of ordinary needle-work is proverbial.
The cramped posture, the strain of the eyes, the derangement
of the digestive organs, lungs, and the nerves, over a monoto-
nous task, have told in fearful effects upon the health and
character of needlewomen. The best medical opinion is, that
the exercise of the lower limbs in operating the machine is
highly invigorating.

The following figures, showing the number of machines sold
by WHEELER & WILSON, indicate the extent and increase of
their business for seven years : 1853, 799 machines; 1854,
956; 1855, 1171; 1856, 2210; 1857, 4591; 1858, 7978:
7859, 21,306. Their sales now exceed the combined sales of
all other manufacturers in the United States.

The small shop of this Company in Watertown in 1852,
turning out eight or ten machines per week, and an obscure
office of one room on the second floor, contrast strongly in
1861 with the manufactory at Bridgeport, Ct., covering an
area of nearly four acres of ground, driven by immense steam-
power, employing an army of mechanics, capable of turning
out 500 machines per day (of a capacity greater than all the
armories of the United States, and equalling them in the completeness of its appointments), and the office and sales-room,
No. 505 Broadway, extending 200 feet, and rivalling in finish
and adornment the halls of royalty, and visited by ladies of
the highest social position, with agencies in the principal places
throughout the country, and in all the capitals of the civilized
world.

There is, too, a corresponding contrast between the machines manufactured by this Company now, and those made in 1852. Although not radically changed in operation, their range of application has been greatly extended, and for completeness of adaptation for family sewing, and for manufacturers in the same range of purpose and material, nothing further is desired. The successive application of the improved tension and loop-check, the hemmer, marker, binder, corder, and transparent cloth-presser, shows the disposition of this Company to give the public the benefit of all the improvements that mechanical genius produces; while the machine vies in artistic finish with the piano in the boudoir. This machine is unrivalled for—

1. Beauty and excellence of stitch alike upon each side of the fabric sewed.
2. Strength, firmness, and durability of seam, that will not rip nor ravel, and made with
3. Economy of thread.
4. Its attachments and wide range of application to purposes and materials.
5. Compactness and elegance of model and finish.
6. Simplicity and thoroughness of construction.
7. Speed, ease of operation and management, and quietness of movement.

The lock-stitch made by this machine cannot be ravelled, and presents the same appearance upon each side of the seam, a single line of thread extending from stitch to stitch. It is formed with two threads, one upon each side of the fabric, and interlocked in the centre of it. In beauty and regularity, and in the firmness of the seam formed, it excels hand-sewing.

The efficacy of this machine is equal to about ten hands. The WHEELER & WILSON COMPANY has prepared tables showing, by actual experiments of four different workers, the time required to stitch each part of a garment by hand, and with their sewing-machine. Subjoined is a summary of several of the tables:—

	BY MACHINE.		BY HAND.	
	Hours.	Minutes.	Hours.	Minutes.
Gentlemen's Shirts.	1	16	14	26
Frock Coats	2	38	16	35
Satin Vests.	1	14	7	19
Linen Vests.	0	48	5	14
Cloth Pants.	0	51	5	10
Summer Pants.	0	38	2	50
Silk Dress.	1	13	8	27
Merino Dress	1	4	8	27
Calico Dress.	0	57	6	37
Chemise.	1	1	10	31
Moreen Skirt.	0	35	7	28
Muslin Skirt.	0	30	7	1
Drawers.	0	28	4	6
Night Dress.	1	7	10	2
Silk Apron.	0	15	4	16
Plain Apron.	0	9	1	26

NUMBER OF STITCHES MADE PER MINUTE.

	By Hand.	With Machine.	Ratio.
Stitching Fine Linen	23	640	28
" Satin	24	520	22
" Silk	30	550	18
Seaming Fine Cloth	38	594	16
Patent Leather, fine Stitching	7	175	25
Fitting Ladies' Gaiters	28	510	18
Stitching Shoe Vamps	10	210	21
Binding Hats	33	374	11

When the machines are driven by power, the ratio is much higher—1500 to 2000 stitches per minute not being an unusual average.

Seams of considerable length are ordinarily sewed with the best machines at the rate of a yard a minute, and that, too, in a manner far superior to hand-sewing.

The importance of the sewing-machine to the manufacturing interests of the United States is estimated at $342,000,000 annually. The annual saving by the machine is estimated on

Men's and Boys' Clothing in New York city	$7,500,000
Hats and Caps	462,500
Shirt Bosoms	832,750
Boots and Shoes in Massachusetts	7,500,000

It has revolutionized thirty-seven distinct departments of manufactures, and in no branch of sewing can it be dispensed with where time and health are regarded.

The value of the imports of the free states during the fiscal year 1858-9, was $169,162,776; and the exports were $295,812,869. The imports of the slave states were $187,286,786, and the exports $31,985,680. Of the exclusive southern product, the exports from the United States were as follows: Cotton, $161,434,943; tobacco, $21,074,038; sugar, $574,869; molasses, $75,699; spirits from molasses, $760,889; tar, $141,058; rosin and turpentine, $2,248,281; rice, $2,207,148.

Miss Susan Nipper, who lives in a snug tenement alone, was quite flustrated, the other morning, by an early call from a bachelor neighbor. "What do you come here after?" said she. "I came for a match," says he, in the meekest manner possible. "Why don't you make a match?" says she, "I know what you're come for," cried the apparently exasperated virgin, as she backed him into a corner, "you're come here to hug and kiss me almost to death! But you shan't, without you're the strongest, and Lord knows you are!"

VIEW OF BERLIN AND JONES'S FACTORY (No. 1).

ENVELOPES.—THEIR HISTORY, USES, PROGRESS OF MANUFACTURE, &c.

> Go, ring the bells, and fire the guns,
> And fling the starry banner out;
> Shout "Freedom" till your lisping ones
> Give back their cradle shout.
>
> WHITTIER.

Envelopes, as postal packages, came into use in Great Britain after the Act of Parliament, August 17th, 1839, regulating the postage by weight instead of the number of pieces. Their extreme availability was early detected in this country, but our postal laws were then hampered with the absurd regulation of charging for number of pieces instead of by weight; this was done away with by Act of Congress, July 1st, 1845.

In 1843, the first envelope manufactory was established in New York, by a Mr. Pierson, by hand process, using little or no machinery. The process was so slow as to make the cost too great, consequently the business did not prosper, and was abandoned for a time.

In 1847, Jacob Berlin, a man of sagacity and enterprise, bought out Pierson, and commenced the manufacture on a large scale, and with more improved modes, at 180 Fulton street, New York; but still the business did not prosper, and for a time he was discouraged. But by energy and perseverance he at length succeeded in awakening the public attention to their convenience and utility, since which time the business has continually increased.

In 1853, Jacob Berlin retired, and was succeeded by Wm. G. West and H. C. Berlin, who constantly increased their manufacturing facilities till, in 1856, Mr. West also retired, and the present firm of BERLIN & JONES was formed.

In May, of that year, the new firm, to accommodate its immense business, moved its salesrooms to 134 William street, where they still remain, commanding and directing a heavy trade. So greatly had the business increased in 1857, as to compel the removal of the factory to more spacious premises up-town (see cut 1), where they have facilities for producing 400,000 per day, or 140,000,000 per year, of every size, quality, and kind known in the trade, as Business, Legal, Document, Detector, Embossed, Opaque Silvered, Wedding, Mourning, Drug, Pay, Cloth-lined, and Business-illustrated envelopes, together with a very large variety of Union envelopes, Lithograph, Comic, and the ordinary Flag styles, at from two dollars per thousand upwards. At the salesroom, a stock of from fifteen to twenty *millions* is always kept on hand to answer any demand. Orders come from all parts of the Union, the Canadas and Provinces, South America, West Indies, East Indies, and even from Europe. Prices vary, of course, with quality, size, &c.,—running from sixty cents to sixty dollars per thousand. So steady has been the demand, that even during the "panic" (1857-8) this manufactory did not discharge any of their regular hands.

As the process of manufacturing is very interesting, we will here briefly advert to it:—A fine steel cutter, or die, does the work of cutting, the steam power applied being a two-horse power, which forces the cutter through from three hundred to

VIEW OF GUMMING ROOM (NO. 2).

five hundred sheets at one application. These sheets are made of specific surfaces for special kinds and sizes of envelopes, so that in cutting them there may be very little waste. When cut, the open form of the envelope is carried to the "gummer," who gums the lappets with the adhesive, generally made of dissolved gum Arabic. A good hand will gum from fifty to sixty thousand per day.

After gumming, the still open envelopes are placed in a series of sliding shelves to dry. By the aid of hot air applied through steam pipes, the drying occupies but a few moments. They are then borne to the folding machine, through which

VIEW OF FOLDING ROOM (NO. 3).

they are passed with great rapidity, coming out perfectly shaped and closed, ready for the counter's hands, who counts and bands them into packages of twenty-five, after having discarded

VIEW OF FOLDING MACHINE (NO 4).

any that may not be perfectly folded and finished. With every second of time, an envelope must be fed to the insatiate arms which extend to receive it, then withdrawn into the machine where the side and bottom flap are pasted and folded over with unerring precision, and pressed down to a perfect point upon the three impinging edges—the fourth flap being folded over, but left unsealed. This is all done in a mere moment of time, and the envelope drops upon the table before the counter, ready for the bands and packing-box. Twenty-five are put in a package, and twenty packages in a box—making five hundred in each box.

The imperfect from any cause are laid aside, and afterwards sorted, packed, and sold as inferior quality. There is a counting apparatus attached to the folding-machine; but as it counts both good and bad, it is not used, as the manufacturers allow no imperfect work to go out as perfect.

The quantity of paper consumed in the manufacture is enormous. A large number of mills make paper exclusively for this business, employing many hundreds of people and heavy capital. The firm of BERLIN & JONES, alone, consume from five to *ten tons* of mill paper per week, in their business! This amount is sometimes much exceeded, as in the case of heavy extra orders.

The trade, living at a distance, who require supplies, in any amount, have only to write to the manufacturers (Messrs. BERLIN & JONES, No. 134 William street, New York), for samples and accompanying prices, when they will be furnished with the samples by which to make any order.

THE SALT TRADE.—The Onondaga Salt Springs have furnished one of the first and permanent elements of business in Oswego. As early as the year 1818, the manufacture and shipments of the article to this port were quite extensive, and constituted the important branch of commercial business in the contracted facilities at that time. In that season, the receipts of salt at Oswego were 36,000 barrels, of which 26,000 barrels went to Lake Erie by portages around Niagara Falls. In 1819, the receipts of salt were 47,000 barrels—the increase of trade thus early commenced on a large ratio; of this amount, 29,000 barrels passed west, and 18,000 barrels went to ports on this lake and the river St. Lawrence. At this period, the freight on salt from Salina to Oswego was fifty-two cents per barrel; warehouse charges at Oswego five cents; from Oswego to Lewiston thirty-one cents; and by the portages around the Falls to Black Rock fifty-two cents—making the cost of transporting the article from Salina to Black Rock, or Fort Erie on the Niagara River, $1.40 per barrel, $9.85 per ton. The price of salt at Oswego at that time ranged at about $1.50 per barrel. Salt now passes from Syracuse to Chicago, or any of the upper lake ports, at eight to thirteen cents per barrel, according to the demand for ballast at Oswego.

"Tom, what in the world put matrimony into your head?"
"Well, the fact is, I was getting short of shirts!"

CLOTHS, CASSIMERES, &c.

"Each climate needs what other climes produce,
And offers something to the general use."

Amongst the many branches of manufacturing industry that have engaged the attention of American capitalists of late years, none is more important and few have made more rapid strides than the manufacture of woollen goods. In 1858, the official returns of this trade gave the following result:

```
Establishments,............................1559
Capital invested,...................   $28,118,650
Raw material used, wool, lbs,..............70,862,829
      "         "     Coal, tons,...........    46,370
Hands employed, males,................    22,678
      "         "     females,................    16,574
Producing an annual value of products of  $13,207,545
```

Most of these goods were for men's wear, and a large portion of them consisted of coarse and light common fabrics, the finer kinds of cloths, cassimeres, doeskins, being mostly imported, but since then we have made a most rapid advance, especially in the latter qualities.

In 1860, it was estimated that the annual product of the woollen factories exceeded $60,000,000, and by means of improved machinery, many of the goods, especially in doeskins and cassimeres, compared favorably with the best products of European looms, and we doubt not in a few years, if the manufacturers will only do as the European manufacturer does, give time and attention to the finishing of their goods, and not be in too great a hurry to take them off their looms and get them into market, we shall be able to produce woollen goods equal in quality to any that Europe can show. At present, however, we have still to import quite largely; the returns of woollens imported in 1860 into the port of New York, alone amounting to nearly $20,000,000.

Amongst the many houses exclusively engaged in the business of cloths, cassimeres, vestings, and goods for men's wear generally, we may mention the firm of SULLIVAN, RANDOLPH & BUDD, late Wilson G. Hunt & Co., as one of the largest and oldest established in the trade. Their beautiful and elegantly constructed warehouses at Nos. 30, 32, 34, and 36 Park Place (corner of Church street), was erected by the firm expressly for their own use at a cost of $85,000, covers an area of 46 by 100 feet, and is five stories high. It is of pure white marble, and is universally admired for its outward architectural beauty and its internal convenience. It is, beyond doubt, one of the most substantially constructed and best arranged warehouses in the country.

This firm have many styles exclusively their own and have the best facilities, both at home and abroad, for obtaining the latest novelties. They have a house in Europe under the management of one of the firm, from whom they are constantly receiving the most desirable goods in the market. Each member of the firm having had many years' experience in the business, and being in connexion with some of the first manufactories of the country, they have obtained facilities that enables them to secure and confine many of the best kinds of cassimeres, vestings, and coatings, to their own sales exclusively.

Merchants, merchant tailors, and clothiers, will always find at this house a large and well-selected stock of cloths, doeskins, cassimeres, vestings, trimmings, and such like articles for men's wear; and the reputation they have acquired during the many years they have been in business, will be a sufficient guarantee that both the price and quality of the articles purchased will be found to compare favorably with any other establishment. We append the card of the house.

SULLIVAN, RANDOLPH & BUDD,

SUCCESSORS TO

WILSON G. HUNT & CO.

Importers and Commission Merchants,

GOODS FOR MEN'S WEAR,

NOS. 30, 32, 34, AND 36 PARK PLACE,

N. SULLIVAN.
P. F. RANDOLPH.
W. A. BUDD.
} **NEW YORK.** {
J. F. HALSTED.
W. V. BROKAW.
J. H. CLARK.

A new motive power has just been tried with success in Paris:—an engine that dispenses with boiler, chimney, and the usual accessories, and economizes besides a saving of over 30 per cent. in steam. The machine utilizes the expansion caused in cold air by the spark of induction in a proper volume of hydrogen.

"Marriage," said an unfortunate husband, "is the churchyard of love."

"And you men," replied the not less unhappy wife, "are the grave-diggers."

AGRICULTURAL IMPLEMENTS.

Crowns have their compass, length of days their date,
Triumphs their tomb, felicity her fate;
Of naught but earth can earth make us partaker,
But knowledge makes a king most like his Maker.
SHAKSPEARE.

Man's inventive genius has during the last few years been highly prolific in producing many rare and ingenious specimens of labor-saving machines, but in no direction, we think, has that genius been so productive of real genuine benefit as in the production of the various machines now in successful use by the farmer and planter. As agriculture affords occupation to nearly three-fourths of the population of the United States, and employs as much capital as all other pursuits combined, it is natural that the mind of the inventor should be attracted towards it as opening a large field for his genius to work upon, and hence the production of the steam-plough, the harvester, the cultivator, the threshing-machine, corn-sheller, and others too numerous to mention.

In the purchase of agricultural implements it is especially desirable that farmers do not incur more expense than is absolutely necessary for the proper management of the farm; but at the same time it will be well to bear in mind that the oft repeated assertion that the "best is the cheapest" will, as heretofore, be found a perfect truism. Farmers, however, are not the only persons interested in this matter. Country merchants are equally so; for, if they desire the prosperity of their respective neighborhoods, they will take pleasure in introducing any invention that promises to be productive of general benefit, remembering always that what they see on their periodical visits to the large cities their neighbors at home have not the opportunity of knowing anything about unless introduced to their notice by themselves.

Two machines, the invention of the last few years, deserve the particular attention of the practical farmer, viz. Whitcomb's Spring-Tooth Horse-Rake, and Kirby's Combined Reaper and Mower.

Whitcomb's Rake overcomes all objections, and is particularly adapted for raking hay on the light porous soil of the prairies, as the teeth pass lightly over without ploughing into the soil. It is a superior rake for gleaning grain fields, as the teeth are gauged in a moment so as to pass just above the surface of the ground, taking up the grain clear from dirt and stones, and will be found valuable in gleaning after the Harvester. It is simple in construction, and will rake from fifteen to twenty acres of hay per day easier than any other rake.

The distinctive feature of Kirby's Combined Reaper and Mower, and that which renders this Harvester the best in the market, is *their ability to work on rough ground*, which is accomplished by the *independent action of the finger bar*, which freely rises and falls in following the inequalities of the ground independently of the driving-wheel. This independent action gives the machine so many advantages on smooth as well as rough ground that it has distanced all other machines, which will soon have to be abandoned. Indeed, they are now being *offered for sale at anything they will fetch*, as farmers who have seen or used Kirby's Harvester will not have any other.

The agents in New York for both these machines are Messrs. GRIFFING, BRO. & Co., who invite farmers and planters to inspect them at their store, the North River Agricultural and Seed Warehouse, No. 60 Cortlandt street, New York, where they have constantly on hand every description of Ploughs, Harrows, Cutters, Fans, Spades, Hoes, and other farm implements, together with the best assortment of Seeds, selected from the best growers with the utmost care. They would also especially call the attention of farmers to their No. 1 PERUVIAN GUANO, which they warrant to be genuine, as purchased from the Peruvian Government Agents. So many frauds have been practised of late years in this article, by the mixing of worthless guano or earth with the genuine and then packing it in second-hand guano bags filled to the weight corresponding with the government stamp upon them, that farmers cannot be too cautious in making their purchases. They will find the genuine article, at the lowest market price, at GRIFFING, BROTHER & Co., 60 Cortlandt street, New York, who are the largest dealers in it in the city. They have also always on hand Land Plaster, Ground Bone, Superphosphate of Lime, and other fertilizers.

In addition to the great coal fields of Pennsylvania, 15,400 square miles, Illinois and Virginia possess together 65,000; while Kentucky and Ohio furnish 34,400 square miles of undeveloped coal, and Southern and Western States yield 27,100. All Europe together has only 17,400 square miles of coal surface, of which 11,850 belong to Great Britain, and of the 40,000,000 tons annually produced there, only 6,918,195 tons were exported last year.

The effect of climate on the human system is shown in a striking manner by the inhabitants of Australia, who in the course of two or three generations lose the corpulent character of Englishmen, and become a tall, gaunt, rawboned race, like the inhabitants of our Southern States.

THE ART INSTITUTIONS.

THE DUSSELDORF GALLERY, removed to 625 Broadway, has for some years past been a popular resort for the lovers of the fine arts. Its collection embraces the works of many great masters.

THE BRYAN GALLERY, OR GALLERY OF CHRISTIAN ART, which is situated on the corner of Broadway and Thirteenth-street, contains a very valuable collection of original pictures of high merit.

THE NATIONAL ACADEMY OF DESIGN, directed and controlled by an association of artists and amateurs, have an annual exhibition of the works of living artists, during the months of April, May, and June.

THE FREE FINE ART GALLERY OF MESSRS. WILLIAMS, STEVENS & WILLIAMS, 353 Broadway, is likewise worthy of notice, from the fact that it contains at all times a rich collection of pictures, engravings, and other works.

CHESS AND BILLIARD SALOONS.

The popularity into which the truly rational and intellectual games of billiards and chess have grown within the past few years is fully evidenced in New York by the large number of places which have been exclusively appropriated to these scientific amusements. For the benefit of those seeking recreation of this character, we name a few only of the leading establishments.

PHELAN'S BILLIARD SALOONS.—The proprietor of these saloons is extensively known throughout the country as the inventor and patentee of "Phelan's Billiard Tables and Combination Cushions;" and his knowledge of the beautiful art, both practical and theoretical, is supposed to excel that of any man now living. This attractive establishment is located at No. 786 Broadway, and is daily visited by gentlemen of distinction from all parts of the world. It combines three spacious rooms, 110 by 50 feet, fitted up in an elegant manner, and provided with thirty tables of the most approved construction.

There are many other large and attractive billiard saloons, of highly respectable character, among which we name:

HONE HOUSE, corner Great Jones street and Broadway, four tables.

COLUMBIA ROOMS, P. D. Kilduff, proprietor, 946 Broadway, nine tables.

UNION SQUARE ROOMS, C. O'Connor, proprietor, 60 and 62 East Fourteenth street, twenty-two tables.

PHELAN'S ROOMS, corner Tenth street and Broadway, M. Phelan, proprietor, twenty-seven tables.

LAFAYETTE HALL, opposite Metropolitan Hotel, Broadway, John Cleveland, superintendent, ten tables.

REEVES' ROOM, 214 Broadway, Captain Reeves, proprietor, eleven tables.

KAVANAGH & FREEMAN, 140 Fulton street, five tables.

BILLIARD HALL, 14 and 16 Fourth avenue, Peter Braisted, proprietor, eight tables.

HIGGINS' ROOM, corner 57th street and Third avenue, two tables.

ROBERTS' ROOM, "Times" Building, Mr. Roberts, proprietor, five tables.

EPPSTEIN'S ROOM, Fourth avenue, cor. 19th street, four tables.

———

In all matters, except a little matter of the tongue, a woman can generally *hold her own.*

AMUSEMENTS AND POPULAR RESORTS.

New York is the headquarters of theatres, concerts, lectures, and miscellaneous enjoyments, and affords to pleasure seekers every opportunity for the gratification of their peculiar tastes. With a view of facilitating the operations of strangers visiting New York in pursuit of enjoyment, we propose briefly to point out some of the prominent and legitimate places of resort, leaving each one, of course, to follow the bent of his inclinations. We commence with the

THEATRES.

In no other city in the world than New York can theatrical entertainments be enjoyed with as much satisfaction. Spectacles are put upon the stage utterly regardless of expenditure, while the performers employed comprise the highest talent of our own country, as well as that of Europe. Among the many magnificent temples dedicated to the drama, we enumerate LAURA KEENE's VARIETIES, located at 622 Broadway. This establishment is justly celebrated for the beauty of its interior arrangements, the excellence of its company, and for the superb manner in which its productions are placed upon the stage.

WALLACK's THEATRE (now the Broadway Music Hall), at 485 Broadway, is well conducted, and a favorite resort.

NIBLO's GARDEN, in Broadway, corner of Prince street, has always been a very fashionable resort. It is capable of containing two thousand persons, and its interior arrangements bespeak much taste and elegance.

THE WINTER GARDEN is a magnificent structure, situated at 641 Broadway.

BOWERY THEATRE is at 46 Bowery.

New Bowery, in the Bowery, above Canal-street.

Barnum's American Museum is on the corner of Broadway and Ann street.

The National Theatre is in Chatham street, near Roosevelt.

Laura Keene's Theatre, 624 Broadway.

Besides these, there are, a French Theatre at 585 Broadway, and several German theatres in the Bowery, the principal one of which is known as the "Stadt Theatre."

The Academy of Music, or Italian Opera House, is situated on the corner of Fourteenth street and Irving Place. During the operatic season the highest order of foreign talent is employed, at salaries which would almost seem to preclude the possibility of rendering it a source of profit to its manager; but the enterprise thus far has been well sustained.

Canterbury Music Hall, 585 Broadway.

The Melodeon Concert Hall, 539 Broadway. One of the most popular resorts for general entertainment in New York.

CUBA.

The population of Cuba is estimated at 1,130,000, of which nearly 550,000 are white inhabitants, 180,000 free colored, 400,000 slaves, and 38,000 Asiatics and Indians. The sugar estates are immensely productive. Twenty-three of the principal plantations, comprising about 100,000 acres of land and 10,175 slaves, are valued at $15,000,000. These twenty-three estates produced, in 1859, 235,000 boxes, the worth of which was four dollars each box, making in all $4,700,000. There are sixteen hundred sugar plantations in Cuba, the exported products of which amount to $50,000,000 per annum.

MAW & CO.'S TILES FOR FLOORS.

> Not enjoyment, and not sorrow,
> Is our destined end or sway;
> But to act that each to-morrow
> Finds us further than to-day.
>
> LONGFELLOW.

Of the many attempts to meet modern architectural requirements in the production of a paving material capable of combining appropriate design with extreme hardness and consequent durability, few have hitherto succeeded so as to bear comparison with the finest specimens of ancient tesselated work, or with its more useful mediæval representative, the *Geometrical Mosaic*, known as *Opus Alexandrinum*, of which numerous interesting examples are still extant, not only as pavements, but on the interior and exterior surfaces of walls, in panels, tablets, pilasters, plinths, pedestals, string-courses, friezes, &c., on edifices bearing date from the time of Constantine the Great down to a comparatively modern period. The great beauty of such fragmentary illustrations of the art as time has spared leads us to regret those technical imperfections which have induced the destruction of an infinite number of graceful examples. It is, on this account, truly unfortunate that the materials generally composing them were either too soft to wear or too hard to work into tesseræ of correct form.

By the application of modern science, both chemical and mechanical, to peculiarly suitable mineral materials, MAW & Co. are not only enabled to produce tesseræ free from either of the ancient imperfections of softness of texture or inaccuracy of outline, but manufacture forms which the materials of the ancient pavements rendered almost unattainable.

With regard to the question of cost and economy, it must

be borne in mind that MAW & Co.'s pavements are as durable as the building of which they form in every respect a consistent portion. *They are more easily kept clean than any other kind of floor*, and entail no subsequent expense for those perishable ornamental and protective coverings, the frequent renewal of which in a few years involves an outlay exceeding the price of a choice specimen of mosaic.

These tiles are adapted to *halls, porches, porticoes, passages, conservatories, footpaces, gangways, verandas, balconies, hearths*, exterior and interior *wall panels, tablets, plinths, skirtings, pedestals, pilasters, string-courses, risers of steps, friezes*, &c., and while being as durable as marble, are capable of a variety of combinations of color unattainable in marble, and of a variety in pattern which could only be furnished in marble at three or four times the expense. Of the advantages of tiles over oil-cloth for vestibules and halls it is only necessary to say, that in addition to the greater facility of cleaning them, and the fact that the wear never obliterates the pattern or affects the surface, the necessity of renewing an oil-cloth within two or three years makes the expense of covering the floor more than the original cost of a beautiful tile pavement, which never requires renewing or repairing.

The interest manifested in the manufacture of tiles is shown by the increasing demand for them, which has been so great as to oblige the manufacturers to double the size of their works (already the largest in the world) during the last year. A brief account of the manufacture may be appropriate in this connexion.

The manufacture consists of two distinct branches, which are essentially different in nearly the whole of their processes. Firstly, the making of encaustic tiles, or those inlaid with a pattern of two colors, which is the reproduction of an art limited in mediæval times to church decorations, but now having a much more extended application. Secondly, the manufacture of plain tiles and tesseræ of a uniform color used in the construction of geometrical mosaic pavements, similar in character to those found in the mediæval buildings in Italy; also moresque and tesselated mosaics similar to those occurring in Pompeii and almost all Roman remains in England and on the continent. The materials employed in both processes are nearly identical, and consist for the most part of the clays and marls of the Shropshire coal-measures, England. These, without any coloring matter, together with the clays from the south of England, form the red, buff, and fawn-colored tiles; and, in connection with different proportions of oxides of iron and manganese, the black, chocolate, and grey tiles. The white, and all the richer colored tiles and tesseræ, are formed of a species of porcelain or parian, the white left uncolored, and the blues and greens covered with oxides of chrome and cobalt. The preparation of what is technically called the body of the tile, which is the first process in the order of manufacture, consists in mixing the constituent clays and other materials with water, and commingling and purifying them by passing them in a semi-liquid state through a sieve made of the finest lawn, containing between 10,000 and 15,000 perforations to the square inch. All the coarse particles are by this means removed, and the texture of the clay rendered perfectly fine and even, as well as greatly adding to the brilliancy of the color. The semi-liquid purified clay is then dried on what is termed the slip-kilns, if for the manufacture of encaustic or inlaid tiles, to a plastic state; or for plain or self-colored tiles, perfectly dry and hard. It is at this point that the two processes diverge and are essentially different; but as the space of this article will not permit a detailed account of the subsequent processes, it merely remains to mention, to those who are interested in statistics, that the manufacture consumes every year about 1500 tons of coal, and from 1100 to 1200 tons of clay, and various materials entering into the composition of the tiles, out of which between 20,000 and 30,000 square yards of tiles, tesseræ, and mosaics are manufactured, composed of 700 or 800 distinct shapes, sizes, and colors. A considerable proportion is sent to America, India, and the Colonies. Among the principal works, Maw & Co. have executed, or have in hand abroad, are the pavements of the entrance hall of the new University of Toronto; also nearly the whole of Osgoode Hall, Toronto, laid by their own men sent out for the purpose; the entrance hall of the Hong Kong Club; deck-house and other parts of the steam yacht *Saïd*, for the Pasha of Egypt; Jessore Church, Bengal; the ground floor of the new General Post-Office, Calcutta; and the Cathedral of Spanish town, Jamaica. The tiles are especially suitable for warm climates in providing cool floors, and at the same time are not too cold in northern latitudes, as from the nature of the material the heat is retained for a long time when the house is warmed.

Messrs. Maw & Co. have an agency at No. 93 Liberty street, New York, where specimens of their manufacture may be seen, and where any information, price lists, and specimen books can be obtained by addressing Charles D. Gambrill, agent.

Several important improvements in the construction of wet gas-meters have been adopted in England, which are said to render them accurate indicators of the quantity of gas passed through them without regard to any variation of the water level. It is now well known that the common American meters are not accurate indicators of the quantity of gas that passes through them.

LIFE INSURANCE.

> Art is long, and time is fleeting,
> And our hearts, though stout and brave,
> Still, like muffled drums are beating
> Funeral marches to the grave.
> LONGFELLOW.

So much has been written about Life Insurance and so many people have experienced the benefits of it, that we shall content ourselves on the present occasion with simply giving the recorded opinion of two most eminent men, and a few reasons why every one having family connexions should avail himself of its benefits.

The late Lord Lyndhurst, Chancellor of England, said: "A policy of Life Insurance is always an evidence of prudent forethought, and no man with a dependent family is free from reproach if his life is not insured, it is the exercise not only of *prudence* but *benevolence* as well." Prof. de Morgan, in his opinion of Life Insurance Companies, concludes, " On the whole, we cannot consider these institutions in any other light than as great public benefits, of which almost any class may avail themselves with advantage to their rising families." Independently of such opinions from such high authorities, Life Insurance is a prudential measure in view of securing peace of mind, not only in sickness, but in native business life. Again—we believe many men in limited circumstances have had their lives sacrificed to anxiety of mind. When taken sick they would not send for a doctor or take the necessary remedies because they could not afford it—they had made no provision for their wives or little ones and could not bear to spend money, which in the event of their death would be so much needed—had they appropriated a small sum yearly in paying for a life policy, how much racking anxiety would be spared them.

In a business point of view it possesses equal advantages, it is a sum of money yearly put out at interest, and should death deprive a man of his family, can always be sold for nearly the amount paid on it. It is also useful as a collateral in business transactions.

One thing must always be borne in mind in effecting an Insurance, that is to see it done in an office whose system of business and standing is a guarantee of security and prompt payment of losses. In this respect, amongst the many to be found in New York, the Connecticut Mutual Life Insurance Company of Hartford is one of the oldest and amongst the first in extent of business.

This Company, organized in 1846, on a system entirely *Mutual*, furnishes Insurance in all the various forms, and to meet all the various contingencies for which Life Insurance is desired, at the *actual cost* to the policy holder. There is no *Stock* or *Guaranty Fund*, to absorb the profits, but all the *surplus* is annually allocated to the policy holders, in proportion to the amount of the premium they pay, and may be appropriated to the payment of *renewal* premiums, after the first four years.

It offers *abundant* security, in a large accumulated Fund, derived from Premiums, amounting to over *Three and a Half Millions*.

Its economy in the management of business permits large dividends to policy holders, which have averaged 50 per cent. per annum.

Its Dividends are annual, and are paid *during the life* of the assured, in cash to those who pay their premiums in cash, or applied in cancelling the notes of those who pay their premium partly by note. Nearly $200,000 have been thus refunded to policy holders during the past year.

It is prompt in payment of losses.

It has few directors, and these are always at their post at weekly meetings. It has an auditing committee appointed yearly, who meet and check the accounts weekly, thus affording every safeguard to insure the policy holders from loss, and the extent of its business may be imagined from the fact, that during last year 1735 policies were issued from the office. The annual exhibit for the year ending January 31, 1861, shows the following gratifying result:

Balance per Statement, Jan. 31st, 1860,			$3,370,001.87
Amount received for Premiums during the year,	$815,711.26		
Amount received for Interest during the year,	261,427.15		
Total Receipts for the year,		$1,077,138.41	
Deduct paid Salaries, Medical Examinations, Advertising, Printing, Stationery, Taxes, Exchange, &c.,	$33,400.67		
Deduct paid Commissions to Agents,	50,053.19		
Deduct paid Losses on 95 Policies, (89 lives,) including $34,700 losses of previous years,	223,400.00		
Deduct paid for Surrendered Policies,	5,335.31	$312,189.17	$764,949.24
			$4,134,951.11
Deduct paid Dividends during the year,		$199,551.00	
Deduct for Notes on Policies cancelled,		45,988.76	
			$245,539.76
Net Balance January 31st, 1861,			$3,889,411.35

Losses on 13 Policies not yet due, $29,480.42

ASSETS.

Loans on Bond and Mortgage of Real Estate,	$2,339,824.65
Loans on Bank Stock and Mortgage Bonds,	64,529.14
Bank and Railroad Stock,	47,955.00
Mortgage Bonds,	41,680.00
United States Coupon Bonds,	45,221.00
Cash deposited in Bank,	69,093.66
Premium Notes on Policies in force,	1,259,734.77
Premiums in the hands of Agents and in transit,	21,373.13
Total Assets	$3,889,411.35
Amount of Losses during the year, 89 lives, (95 Policies.)	217,500.00
Total amount of Losses paid to date,	2,499,461.77
Total amount of Dividends paid to date,	1,757,243.00

Total No. Deaths since organization of the Company, 1,168.
Number of Policies issued during the year, 1,725.
Total number of Policies in force, 10,461.

Should any of our readers desire further information, we refer them for full particulars of rates, and to obtain blanks for the different form of Insurance, pamphlets, reports, &c., to the Agent in New York.

W. S. DUNHAM,
Conn. Mutual Life Insurance Company,
104 Broadway.

OFFICERS.

JAMES GOODWIN, *President,*   Z. PRESTON, *Vice-President.*
GUY R. PHELPS, *Secretary.*

Young ladies who faint on being proposed to, may be readily restored by whispering in their ears that you were only joking.

THE TWINE, CORDAGE, AND PAPER BUSINESS.

> Man loves knowledge, and the beams of truth,
> More welcome touch his understanding's eye,
> Than all the blandishment of sound his ear,
> Than all of taste his tongue.
> AKENSIDE.

The increase in the manufacture of these articles has been most extraordinary; but a few years ago a large portion of our twine and cordage was imported, now we can manufacture sufficient for home consumption and export as well.

We have before us the catalogue of Messrs. WILLARD HARVEY & Co., established twenty years ago at 84 Maiden Lane, and still remaining there and also at 17 Cedar street, who have, during the whole of that time, given their particular attention to this branch of their business, and some idea of the extent the trade has attained may be formed by the enumeration of the different articles with the number of varieties manufactured by them. Under the head of CORDAGE, we have Manilla hemp rope, all sizes; Manilla spun yarn; the best Manilla bed cords; fine Manilla yarn; Jute hemp rope, two sorts various sizes; bright jute bed cords; American hemp rope, four kinds; Russia hemp lines, twelve kinds; Cotton rope, &c., ten kinds all sizes. Packing for steam-engines, tarred, ratlin, and spun yarn, fancy cordage, welting cord, whip cord and clock cord, hatters' cord, seaming cord, masons' lines, &c., &c.

In SEINE TWINES there are three different kinds of various numbers. Gilling threads of all colors and numbers; while of fishing lines the variety is almost endless, and saddlers' and shoe threads, twelve varieties. In twines which they denominate "Star Twines," there are thirty-two varieties of various threads, and put up in all usual size balls and packages. Besides which, they manufacture hemp twines, spring twine, paper twine, baling twine, broom-winding twine, wool twine, bottling twine, sewing twines, Spread Eagle Mills twine, flax sail, and broom sewing twines, &c., &c. They are also sole agents for the American Twine, Thread, and Line Company.

Their stock of all these goods is most complete, they having made this trade peculiarly their own, and having by their long experience discovered exactly what is wanted by the various buyers of these articles, are always prepared to suit them.

Using the best quality of stock, and availing themselves of superior manufacturing facilities, W. H. & Co. have always had the most gratifying testimonials from their customers as to their satisfaction of the way their orders have been furnished; and as a further proof of the superiority of their manufacture it is only necessary to state that the first premiums have invariably been awarded to them by the highest institutions in the country where their goods have been entered for competition.

In the article of paper, we may mention the following of which they have a large stock always on hand, viz. wrapping papers, pure manilla, mixed and inferior manillas; English glazed hardware, American glazed hardware, staple hardware, blasting, cartridge, hosiery, rope and rag; palm leaf, straw, shoe, tea, fine ball, druggists' heavy wrapping, oiled, silk, envelope, fancy and plain cover, tissue, roofing and sheathing, hatters' and pyrotechnic papers.

For printing, they have fine and common news, book, common white, colored medium, pamphlet cover, and white wrapping paper.

For writing, letter paper of all descriptions, bath, post, gilt edged, plain, ruled, and unruled; note papers, staple or fancy, all sizes; commercial paper, thin, ruled or unruled; sermon and foolscap, of all prices and suitable for all purposes, with a varied assortment of boards and envelopes.

In BLOTTING PAPER, a thick firm sheet and known as the "Treasury Blotting Pad," introduced by them, has had many imitators and some even with the pretence of being patented, but they have not come up to the original.

Such is a brief sketch of the principal trade of the house; merchants desiring further information should apply to them for a catalogue, which they will gratuitously furnish. All goods sold by them are warranted, and they bestow their best attention in shipping them, care being always taken to procure the lowest rates of freight and insurance.

As gentlemen, upright and honorable in their business transactions, proven during the long term of twenty years by the liberal patronage they have received, we can confidently commend their establishment to the attention of merchants in all parts of the country.

VALUABLE PRESENTS.—Some one speaking of new year's presents says, "The best thing to give to your enemy is forgiveness; to your opponent, tolerance; to a friend, your heart; to your children, a good example; to your father, deference; to your mother, love; to yourself, respect; to all men, charity; to God, obedience."

THE PAST AND PRESENT.—"New England," says Cotton Mather in 1718, "is now so far improved as to have the best part of two hundred meeting-houses." What would he say now (1859) to find, they are over 6,000?

ALCOHOL, CAMPHENE, &c.

> Honor to him, who, self-complete and brave,
> In scorn can carve his pathway to the grave,
> And, heeding naught of what men think or say,
> Makes his own heart his world upon the way.
>
> BURNS.

Alcohol, as is generally pretty well known, is distilled from whiskey—nine gallons of the latter, making about five of the former. Alcohol for burning fluid is ordinarily ninety-five per cent., while druggists' alcohol is but eighty-four per cent., reduced to that standard after distillation. *Pine oil*, or *camphene*, is distilled from spirits of turpentine, the produce of the forests of North Carolina. This loses in distillation about a gallon in a barrel, or one and one-fourth per cent. Burning fluid is made by the admixture of one gallon of pine oil to four gallons of alcohol. The chief merits of this latter article as a material of light, consist in its brilliancy, cheapness, and far greater cleanliness than either oil or candles; its principal demerit is its liability to explosion. Upon this important point one of our largest manufacturers says:—It has been ascertained that nearly all the accidents attending the use of burning fluid originated either by attempting to fire shavings or other combustible materials with a fluid lamp mostly glass; or by the attempt to fill the lamp while burning. This is by far the most fruitful source of accidents—but thanks to the inventive genius of the American people, several kinds of lamps have been patented, and are now in use, which entirely prevent the possibility of an accident occurring from this cause, for the act of unscrewing the lamp puts out the flame by the action of a spiral spring forcing up an extinguisher which entirely prevents the possibility of accidents. But there are still other improvements.

One is, that the fluid is inclosed in a gutta percha case, so that in case of a glass lamp falling and breaking it cannot possibly ignite. Another is, that the gas and not the fluid is consumed, thereby making a light equal to gas. The introduction of these various improved lamps has rendered the burning of camphene or fluid as safe as any other illuminator.

The large consumption of these articles employs a number of manufactories, amongst the oldest of which is the establishment of J. A. WEBB & Co., 229 and 230 West Street. Mr. Augustus V. H. Webb, the father of one of the present proprietors, claims to be the inventor of camphene, for which he obtained a patent dated the 19th February, 1839, manufacturing then and subsequently in Williamsburgh.

In 1853, Mr. J. A. WEBB succeeded his father in the business, which he continued till 1855, when finding his premises too small for his increasing business, he commenced the erection of the factory in West street. This factory he had built after his own plans, and his long previous experience enabled him to have erected one of the most perfect manufactories of its kind. With his increased facilities he devoted his whole time to the development of his business, which resulted in his effecting many improvements we shall speak of presently.

The building occupies a frontage of seventy-five feet, and is one hundred and fifty feet deep. On the left of the entry way is inclosed the counting-room. Further on, let into the ground is a large reservoir, capable of holding one hundred and thirty-five barrels, into which the whiskey is dumped, and from thence, by means of steam pumps, pumped into the stills. There is another reservoir on the roof of the same capacity. Above and by the side of the reservoir are several pumps, condensers, and receptacles for the pure alcohol. They have here also a very simple and perfect machine for measuring, which is much more accurate than the ordinary gauge.

Separated from this room by a brick wall sixteen inches thick, is the still room, containing one still capable of holding twenty-five hundred gallons, and a smaller one, the whole having a power of production of over one hundred barrels a day. On the roof of the building are the reservoirs, water tanks, condensers, &c., whilst in the rear of the yard is the boiler room, the only place in the factory where fire is allowed; and to prevent the possibility of accident from this source, in the still room is a powerful steam pump, with hose constantly attached, by which the whole building could be instantly deluged with water.

Messrs. WEBB & Co., by constant supervision and strict attention to business, have succeeded in getting their ninety-five per cent. alcohol recognised as the most uniform and purest in the market. They have also, after much labor, perfected a higher grade of spirit, called absolute alcohol, one hundred per cent., warranted free from all foreign substances, fusil oils, water, &c., the highest and most perfectly tasteless spirit ever manufactured, indispensable for druggists, perfumers, &c. They are now introducing a new illuminating oil, made from coal. They have already got this fluid to a very great perfection, so as to command as large a demand as they can conveniently supply. They have got this oil to be almost entirely free from smoke or smell.

The firm of J. A. WEBB & Co. is composed of J. A. WEBB and JEREMIAH BAKER, and for the convenience of their business they have a store at 165 Pearl street, where the books are kept, and the ordinary transactions of the house carried on, to which establishment all orders should be addressed.

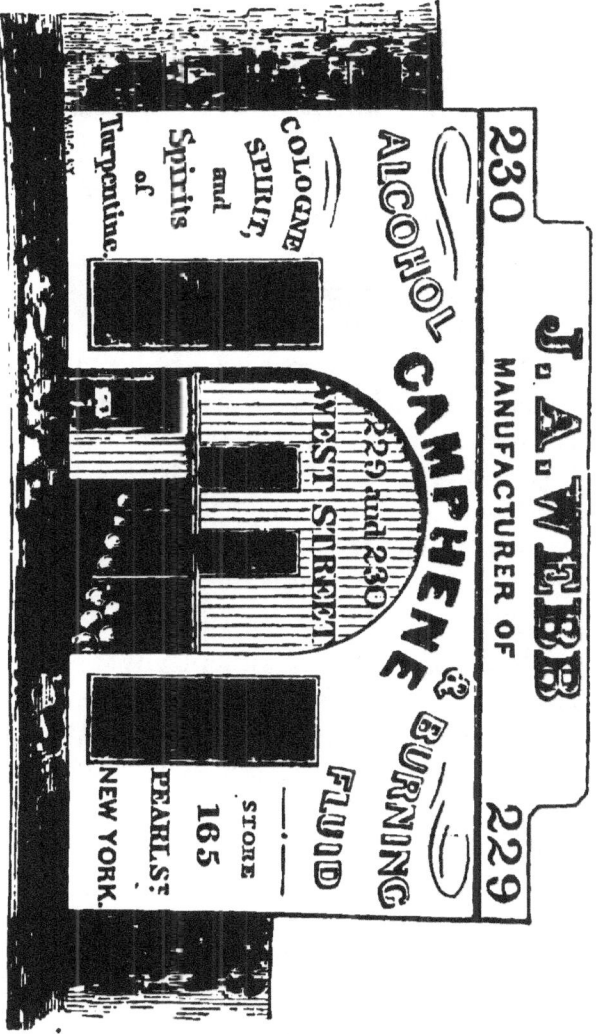

J. A. WEBB & CO.'S CAMPHENE, ALCOHOL, BURNING FLUID, AND ILLUMINATING OIL ESTABLISHMENT.

ONE OF THE INSTITUTIONS OF NEW YORK,

and one that has attained here greater perfection than in any other city on this continent, is its Wine and Ale Vaults. These are a kind of half wholesale and half retail establishments, where one can buy either a glass or a puncheon. The great difficulty of obtaining wines and ales, especially of foreign brand, pure and unadulterated, in small quantities, necessitated their establishment, and they have proved a great success. One of the oldest and largest of these is G. E. MENDUM's, at the corner of Cedar street and Broadway. His place during business hours is constantly crowded, and his men are kept busy drawing ales, of which he keeps the following home and foreign brands always on draught:

Allsopp's East India Tonic Pale Ale.
Bass's East India Tonic Pale Ale.
Younger's Scotch Ale.
Burton "On Trent," 1856.
Gaul's Philadelphia "Golden Ale."
Howard & Fuller's Delicious Spring Water ditto.
Jones's XXX Stock (Brewed from English Malt).
Smith's American Bitter Ale (Brewed in Wheeling, Va.).
Smith's Champagne Ale (The finest ever offered in the U. S.).
Smith's Kennet Ale (Highly recommended to Dyspeptics and Consumptives).
Guinness's world-renowned Dublin Porter.
Murphy's celebrated Cork Porter.
Marr's Saratoga Cream Ale (From the celebrated Saratoga Springs).
Vassar's Imperial Ale, old and fresh.
Gray's Philadelphia XXXX Extra.

They are kept in cool cellars and drawn from the wood, thus

preserving their pure flavor, and many of the ales, being rare productions, cannot be obtained elsewhere on draught. Such a reputation have they obtained for purity and flavor that his retail trade is comparatively small to his bottling business, orders constantly coming in from all parts for wines, liquors, ales, porters, &c., in quantities of a pint to a cask. Besides these he keeps on hand various foreign pickles, sauces, anchovies, caviare, cheese, and other luxuries for the table, and having the best facilities for obtaining them, he has always the choicest the various markets afford.

Strangers visiting New York, appreciating a glass of good ale, or requiring any other of MENDUM's edibles or bibibles, should stop in at the vaults, corner of Cedar street and Broadway, as they will be sure of finding the best there.

Comfort Bennet, the millionaire of Chemung county, is a remarkable man. He went to Big Haho without means, and worked for the farmers for eight years before he had means to buy land. In the meridian of life he lost his right hand. He is now eighty years old, has been blind four years, and has accumulated by earnings and savings, not speculations, a million dollars.

The product of the wheat crop last year in six Northwestern States was 94,000,000 bushels. Illinois and Wisconsin 25,000,000 each; Indiana, 16,000,000; Michigan, 12,000,000; Iowa, 10,000,000; Minesota, 6,000,000. The whole grain crop of Illinois in 1861 is estimated at 101 bushels to each inhabitant.

Woman has found her true "sphere" at last. It is about twenty-seven feet round, made of hoops.

DISTANCES IN THE CITY.

FROM BATTERY.	FROM EXCHANGE.	FROM CITY HALL.	TO
¼ mile.			Rector street.
½	¼ mile.		Fulton.
¾	½		City Hall.
1	¾	¼ mile.	Leonard.
1¼	1	½	Canal.
1½	1¼	¾	Spring.
1¾	1½	1	Houston.
2	1¾	1¼	Fourth.
2¼	2	1½	Ninth.
2½	2¼	1¾	Fourteenth.
2¾	2½	2	Nineteenth.
3	2¾	2¼	Twenty-fourth.
3¼	3	2½	Twenty-ninth.
3½	3¼	2¾	Thirty-fourth.
3¾	3½	3	Thirty-eighth.
4	3¾	3¼	Forty-fourth.
4¼	4	3½	Forty-ninth.
4½	4¼	3¾	Fifty-fourth.
4¾	4½	4	Fifty-eighth.
5	4¾	4¼	Sixty-third.
5¼	5	4½	Sixty-eighth.
5½	5¼	4¾	Seventy-third.
5¾	5½	5	Seventy-eighth.
6	5¾	5¼	Eighty-third.
6¼	6	5½	Eighty-eighth.
6½	6¼	5¾	Ninety-third.
6¾	6½	6	Ninety-seventh.
7	6¾	6¼	One Hundred and Second.
7¼	7	6½	One Hundred and Seventh.
7½	7¼	6¾	One Hundred and Twelfth.
7¾	7½	7	One Hundred and Seventeenth.
8	7¾	7¼	One Hundred and Twenty-first.
8¼	8	7½	One Hundred and Twenty-sixth.

Many persons are in advance of their age, but an old maid generally manages to be about ten years behind hers.

HACKNEY COACH FARES.

AS ESTABLISHED BY LAW.

Distances.	One Passenger.	Each Additional Passenger.
Not exceeding one mile	$ 50	$0 37½
Exceeding one mile and not exceeding two	75	37½
To New Almshouse, and returning	1 00	50
To 40th-street, and remaining half an hour and returning	1 50	50
To 61st-street, and remaining three quarters of an hour and returning	2 00	50
To 86th-street, and remaining one hour and returning	2 50	75
To Harlem, and remaining three hours and returning	5 00	No extra charge for additional passengers.
To High Bridge, and remaining three hours and returning	5 00	
To King's Bridge, and remaining three hours and returning	5 00	

For the use of a coach by the day, with one or more passengers, five dollars.

For the use of a coach by the hour, with one or more passengers, with privilege of going from place to place, and stopping as often as may be required, one dollar per hour..

In all cases where the hiring of a coach is not at the time thereof specified to be by the day or hour, it shall be deemed to be by the mile.

For children between two and fourteen years of age, half price only is to be charged, and for those under two years no charge is to be made.

The baggage to be taken without charge with each passenger, is one trunk, valise, saddle-bags, portmanteau, or box, if he be requested so to do; but for any trunk, or other such articles above named, more than one for each passenger, six cents can be charged.

In case of disagreement, as to the distance or price, the same shall be determined by the Mayor, or Superintendent of Coaches.

No charge can be made unless the number of the carriage is placed on the outside, and the rates of fare in a conspicuous place inside said carriage.

If more than the legal rates are asked, nothing can be collected for services.

A violation of this ordinance subjects the offender to a fine of ten dollars.

NEW LEATHER.—Whale skin has been successfully tanned, and made into good leather. In illustration of the fact that the gelatinous substances compounded of the skin of nearly all animals are capable of being converted into leather, Dr. JULES CLOQUET lately produced at the French Academy of Sciences a pair of boots made of the tanned skin of a boa constrictor. The introduction of the skins of the inferior vertebrata into trade was advocated in the Academy.

A dealer in dry goods, in Paris, has engaged the services of several well dressed ladies, who promenade near his store, and when they see any lady looking into the window, two of them approach and exclaim, "Oh, isn't it sweet!" or "How cheap!—Let us go in and buy it!"

THE MANUFACTURE OF HOOP SKIRTS.

> O woman! dear woman! whose form and whose soul
> Are the light and the life of each spell we pursue;
> Whether sunned in the tropics, or chilled at the pole,
> If woman be there, there is happiness too.
>
> MOORE.

L. A. OSBORN & CO.'S CELEBRATED ESTABLISHMENT.

From reliable data we are enabled to state that 1746 was the era of hoop petticoats. In a quotation of prices of dry goods in those days we find the following articles enumerated:

Hoop Petticoats of five rows,	- - -	.	$1 25
" " six rows,	- -	-	1 55
" " three rows,	- -	-	69
Whalebone Hoop Petticoats,	- -	-	3 75

Who the Osborn was of those days neither history nor tradition has informed us; but hoop petticoats were articles of female attire then as now. Will they be a hundred years hence? Probably they will. The female shape and the female nature are not likely to alter.

The importance of the hoop skirt business as conducted at the present period will appear from the following statement. There are in this city about nine large factories. Some of these employ in their busy seasons as many as eight and nine hundred hands. It is estimated that during their busy seasons, which last about eight months of the year, as many as five thousand dozen (or sixty thousand) hoop skirts are made each day. These, of course, are of all sizes, all patterns, common and fine, and run from five hoops to fifty. The manufacture of these most popular of all fashionable aids to the female figure has very considerably improved within these last few years.

Amongst those who have aided these improvements are Messrs. L. A. OSBORN & Co. These gentlemen occupy, in addition to seven spacious floors on Warren street, being the whole of the large building No. 92, a large building in the upper portion of the city. In these two establishments there is a force of from 800 to 1000 hands, most of whom are young ladies. In addition to these two large establishments, we may add, as being directly and exclusively connected, one large factory for braiding the hoops, in Bridgeport, Ct., two in Paterson, N. J., besides several establishments for making the steel hoops, metal trimmings, &c., in New York, Connecticut, and Massachusetts. With this large force of hands, and the necessary machinery, Messrs. OSBORN & Co. are enabled to produce from 2500 to 4000 skirts per day, for which large number they have a constantly increasing demand. In the various departments of manufacture they use 400,000 yards of steel springs per week, and in the same length of time consume 100,000 yards of tape, a much larger quantity of braid, and 2,000,000 clasps and slides. Mr. OSBORN is well known as the pioneer in extension skeleton hooped skirts, having been the first to introduce them in this country. By his patent, he has the exclusive right to make, use, or sell extension skirts, and from him all other manufacturers derive the privilege of making or using. Osborn's Patent Skirts are formed of a series of hoops, each being cut or parted so as to form two or more adjustable ends, so arranged that the diameter of the skirts may be enlarged or diminished, by connecting the ends of the hoops in such a manner that they will slide towards and from each other, to enlarge and diminish the diameter of the skirt, in combination with belts and cords, crossing the hoops to hold them together; constituting what is known as Ladies' Extension Skeleton Skirts. The other of the aforesaid patents contains three claims.

After patient and persevering effort during three years before the Patent Office, Mr. Osborn obtained, on the second of April last, a valuable patent for making hoop skirts by means of forms or frames, on which the hoops are placed while the workman is fastening them with tapes or cords, so as to make the skirt the shape required. Mr. Osborn had much opposition to contend against before he succeeded in getting it, but he has at length overcome all difficulties, and by means of this patent the firm at 92 Warren street are now enabled to manufacture skirts more durable and perfect in form than can be produced at any other establishment, unless they use his patent, which most manufacturers are glad to pay him for the privilege of using. This last patent is issued under the new law, for seventeen years, during which time, as skirts cannot be made without Osborn's frames, every manufacturer must have a license from him to make them.

THE INVISIBLE DISPATCH.

The plan of writing with rice water, to be rendered visible by the application of iodine, was practised with great success in the correspondence during the late war in India. The first letter of this kind was received from Jellalabad, concealed in a quill. On opening it a small paper was unfolded, on which appeared only a single word, "iodine." The magic liquid was applied, and an important dispatch from Sir Robert Sale stood forth.

It is said that a girl in England was struck dumb by the firing of a cannon. Since then a number of married men have invited the artillery to come and discharge their pieces on their premises.

DRUGS, MEDICINES, AND CHEMICALS.

> This world is like a mint, we are no sooner
> Cast into the fire, taken out again,
> Hammer'd, stamp'd and made current, but
> Presently we are chang'd.
>
> DECKER.

About twenty-six years ago Mr. A. B. SANDS, then just attained to his majority, after having acquired a thorough practical knowledge of the drug business, which he obtained by being in two of the best wholesale and retail drug stores at that time extant; commenced in a very small way retailing drugs and medicines at the corner of William and Fulton streets (on the very spot where Washington Irving was born). He was assisted in this by his brother David, who had then recently graduated at the Medical College, and they both entered on their duties with the determination to succeed if constant application, strict integrity, and great care in the preparation and quality of their articles, could accomplish that result.

At that time there was a large amount of deterioration in the preparation of medicines, but Mr. S. determined that his should be pure, and therefore prepared nothing but from the best raw material. In this he was greatly aided by his brother's knowledge, and succeeded in getting his preparations into public notice, from which time they have had the gratification of seeing them rise step by step higher and higher into public favor.

In 1846 they removed to the corner of Gold and Fulton sts., while their present location was being enlarged, after which they returned to the old spot, where they have since remained.

In such a manner and with such aims Mr. A. B. SANDS commenced the business now carried on under the style of A. B. SANDS & Co. This firm, at the present time, is recognised as one of the most prominent houses in New York for Drugs, Medicines, and Chemicals. With the advantages of their long experience of twenty-six years they have established valuable business connexions with foreign countries, giving them extra facilities for importing crude drugs and other species of merchandize required in their business direct from the places of their production. Their extensive capital enables them to purchase on the best terms, always paying cash, never under any circumstances giving notes, and they therefore can sell on as advantageous terms as any house in the trade.

Their facilities for manufacturing, and their thorough knowledge of the theory and manipulation of drugs and chemicals, together with the purity of these articles, have obtained for their preparations a world-wide celebrity, and they have now constantly employed a force of about thirty hands in putting them up.

Essential Oils and Select Powders are leading features of their business, being of the purest kinds and finest flavors.

They are also the proprietors and manufacturers of the celebrated

Sands' Extract of Sarsaparilla.
McMunn's Elixir of Opium.
Sands' Remedy for Salt Rheum.
Sands' Peruvian Febrifuge, &c., &c.

All of which are well known and deservedly popular remedies.

Their Seidlitz Powders have a universal reputation, orders arriving for them from all parts of the globe; parties having once had these will not be satisfied with any other.

Their Flavoring Extracts, although of comparative recent introduction, have met with great approval, and bid fair to become standard popular favorites.

From little beginnings, twenty-six years ago, the house of A. B.

Sands & Co. has grown to its present magnitude. The strict integrity these gentlemen have ever shown in all their business transactions has gained them hosts of friends, and we can cordially recommend them to all who require any articles they deal in.

A. B. SANDS & CO.

(Late A. B. & D. SANDS & CO.)

IMPORTERS AND WHOLESALE DEALERS IN

DRUGS, MEDICINES AND CHEMICALS,

GLASSWARE, PAINTS, OILS, DYE-STUFFS,

Brushes, Sponges, Soaps, Perfumery, &c.

141 WILLIAM STREET, Cor. of FULTON,

ABRAHAM B. SANDS,
ALEXANDER V. BLAKE.
NEW YORK.

With the aid of machinery twenty-five persons turn out 600 pairs of shoes daily, at a factory at Haverhill, Mass. Every operation, from first to last, even to the final polish, is done by machinery, except fitting the shoes to the last.

A Brute of a Husband.—Wife (anxiously)—"What did that young lady observe who passed us just now?" Husband (with a smile of calm delight)—"Why, my love, she observed rather a good-looking man walking with quite an elderly female—that's all. Ahem!"

Office and Warehouses, Nos. 366 & 368 WASHINGTON ST., and 94, 96, 98 NORTH MOORE ST.,

DOMESTIC LIQUORS.

> Then gently scan your brother man,
>   Still gentler sister woman,
> Though they may gang a kennin wrang,
>   To step aside is human.
>
> BURNS.

The title of our article will, we know, not be attractive to many of our most excellent citizens, who are known as temperance men and tee-totallers; still we hope they will read it, as we mean to put in a plea for domestic liquors in their pure state, as being, taken in moderation, a useful and decidedly necessary article of commerce.

Our limits do not allow an extended argument on the constitution of man, but it is patent to every one, that each individual has his own peculiar idiosyncrasy, varying in degree, and form, and shape. Some show it in the form of excitement, others in their studious and retiring habits. These two classes taken in a generic sense form the world, but they are capable of an immense amount of subdivision. From the first we get our generals, soldiers, sailors, politicians, and most enterprising merchants; from the latter our historians, poets, lawgivers, and philanthropists. Each of these classes is separate and distinct, and yet all possess features in common. When the man of excitement has overworked his animal nature, he wants a stimulant, and it does him good, preventing too great a reaction from sudden repose. When the student has overworked his brain, he takes a stimulant, and that infuses life into his body. In each case they are useful and requisite, provided the liquors taken are pure, benefiting both mind and body when used in moderation. But the difficulty is to get simply the alcoholic rectified liquors, without any admixture of fusil oils or foreign deleterious matter. The one imparts vigor to the system; the other creates a morbid appetite for repetition, which, if indulged in, leads to a slow but sure destruction of both the mental and bodily faculties. We know, from observation, unfortunately too well, that the majority of liquors vended, are composed of poisonous mixtures; and this, in this country, is caused from the great desire of all for foreign liquors. These, to be pure, must command a high price, but the majority drinking them cannot afford to pay it; hence the poisonous mixtures sold under the names of French brandy, Scotch and Irish whiskeys, Holland gin, &c. The shipper abroad, to compete with domestic liquors in this market, adulterates them, and they again receive a further adulteration when they arrive. Besides this, many are made here, of nice flavor, and good imitations of the original, but of the most intoxicating qualities. This almost universal, but foolish and insane desire for foreign liquors, has been the cause of the introduction of delirium tremens and mania à potu into this country, which were never known in former years; then our citizens were content to drink our own home-made whiskey. Now how different; they are of almost daily occurrence. Our farmers in remote places still use the wholesome stimulant made from the pure grain, and live a vigorous life, to a good old age; while our powerful muscular men, living in the large cities, lose their vigor almost in the prime of life. Does not this teach a lesson, and would it not be well for our legislators to turn their attention to it, and by a stringent law prevent the vending of these poisons? Such a law would be the best aid to temperance that could be made; the desire for repetition created by the narcotics and unnatural stimulants of adulterated liquor would be taken away, and although intoxication might still to some extent exist, it would not be anything like as great, or be productive of nearly such baneful consequences.

We have put in this as a hasty plea for pure domestic liquors, but it is only a skeleton of an argument to what might be urged. As we said before, men require stimulants, and will always have them, therefore total abstinence is an impossibility,

JERSEY CITY.

ENTIRE BLOCK—*Bounded by Provost Street, Pavonia Avenue, South First Street, and Hudson River.*

Nos. 360 & 362 GREENWICH STREET, NEW YORK.

ALCOHOL DISTILLERY & SPIRIT REFINERY
360 362
R. HOFFMAN & CURTISS

and will remain ever so, but temperance is not, and may be produced, or at least greatly enhanced, by proper legislation.

Amongst the most prominent distillers and rectifiers of domestic liquors, whose brand is distinguished for purity, stand the firm of HOFFMAN & CURTISS. They have had many years' experience, and have spared neither expense nor pains to make their distillation perfect, and their brands of whiskey from wheat, barley, or rye, have been pronounced unsurpassed. At their distillery in New Jersey, occupying a whole block (see cut No. 2), they ordinarily consume fifteen hundred bushels of grain per day, producing about one hundred and fifty barrels of spirit. This distillery is one of the most perfect of its kind in the States. From thence the spirit is taken to the rectifying house at 362 Greenwich street, N. Y., as represented in cut No. 3. Here it is thoroughly purified, and is then conveyed to the warehouses, at Nos. 366 and 368 Washington street (see our first engraving), in which are stored on the five floors of the building thousands of barrels of whiskey, where they are kept to acquire age, the several floors varying from the new distillation to five years old. We have not entered into a full detail of the process of distillation, as we believe it is pretty generally known, but we would make mention of two articles manufactured by this firm, which deserve especial notice. The first is a superior spirit, perfectly pure, without taste or smell, which they call " Excelsior pure spirits," and which we think must prove invaluable to perfumers and druggists. The other they have patented under the brand of *Hoffman & Curtiss' Superior Excelsior Gin.* This is distilled from rye and barley malt, and the Italian juniper berry, and is equal to the best Holland gin ever imported into this market. The difference between Holland and domestic gin is imputed by Americans to the difference in the two kinds of grain. If so, why did not the American grain exported to Europe during the Russian war, and which was there distilled into gin, impart to it the flavor which characterizes our domestic gin? It did not do so; it was Holland gin to the taste, although manufactured from American grain. The fact is, it is simply a prejudice against domestic manufacture, and whilst the pure Holland and domestic gins are both wholesome beverages in moderation, there is a large amount of impure poison made to be sold at a price to compete with the domestic as real "Holland Gin," which does incalculable mischief. We think Messrs. H. & Co.'s "Excelsior" ought to drive the rubbish from the market.

The articles manufactured by this firm are the following, all warranted pure and free from any deleterious mixture: Pure Spirits, plain; American Brandy; American Gin; Excelsior Gin, equal to Holland Gin; N. E. Rum; Cider Brandy, Excelsior Spirits (distilled), wholly free from flavor; Cologne Spirits, 95 per cent. (flavorless); Alcohol, 95 per cent.; Monongahela Whiskey; Bourbon Whiskey; Clarified Whiskey; Steam Refined Whiskey; Cherry Rum; Cherry Brandy; Cordials, Peppermint, &c.; Wines—Port, Madeira, Sherry, Malaga—made from the imported White and Red Wines, free from any deleterious admixture; American Cognac Brandy, distilled from prunes and ordinary raisins, will be found to compare favorably with the imported Rochelle Cognac Brandy; Burning Fluid, &c.

Of course an establishment of this magnitude gives employment to a considerable number of hands. They have ordinarily in their employ about fifty persons, in the various departments, which number in the busy season is considerably increased. Messrs. Hoffman & Curtiss have spared neither labor nor money in producing the purest and most perfect articles, and they have been rewarded with a high appreciation of their manufacture by consumers, and we can only wish them a continuance and increase of prosperity, hoping before long to see the absurd prejudice against American liquors done away with, as in ninety-nine cases out of one hundred they are far more beneficial than the so-called imported liquors.

A VISIT TO A PIANO FACTORY.

WITH SOMETHING ABOUT THE ORIGIN OF MUSIC AND PIANOS.

──────────── The birds instructed man,
And taught him songs before his art began.
And while soft evening gales blew o'er the plains,
And shook the sounding reeds, they taught the swains,
And thus the pipe was framed, and tuneful reed.

Such was Lucretius's idea of the origin of musical instruments of the inflatile kind as given us in his work on the nature of things, which, if historians do not place much reliance on, has certainly the merit of being very poetical. The same notion concerning wind instruments is found in Ovid's beautiful account of the transformation of the nymph Syrinx into reeds. But Thomas Aquinas in his "Storia della Musica" disdains to follow the example of the heathen author of the "Metamorphoses" or the disciple of Epicurus, and leaves the origin of music to chance; contending that the first man was endowed with every kind of knowledge by the Creator, and that he excelled in music, as well as in all the arts and sciences. Leaving these ingenious guesses and fictions, we find the earliest authentic record of music in the Scriptures, where it is written that Jubal, the seventh in descent from Adam, was the father of such as handle the harp and organ. These terms, however, must not be taken quite literally, but rather in a generic sense signifying all instruments of a stringed and tube kind. Although this is recorded in Genesis, it is pretty certain that the Jews acquired their knowledge of music from the Egyptians, in which country it seems to be pretty well agreed the art originated, and acquired great perfection, as is evidenced by the researches of modern travellers. Bruce found in Thebes a fresco painting of a harp evidently of a very ancient origin. In form, dimensions, and ornament, this instrument might be mistaken for one of modern date, insomuch, that when a drawing was shown of it in London, doubts were thrown on its fidelity. Forty years after, however, M. Denon bore testimony to the truth of Bruce's description, and the accuracy of the sketch, thus evidencing that great proficiency was attained in the art centuries ago.

The origin of the Square Piano Forte does not date back over a century ago; it was the invention of a German mechanic, named Viator, the idea being taken from the Clavichord, but it is only like this latter instrument in its shape, with the same dispositions of strings and keys; in action it is totally dissimilar. The invention was immediately taken up by other makers, who left their Clavichords and Harpsichords for the new instrument, the earliest and largest maker known being Zumpe, who realized a large fortune and retired. The Grand Piano Forte is supposed to be of earlier date than the square, and is variously attributed to a German named Schrœder, and to a harpsichord maker named Christofali, of Padua. The Grand Piano Forte retains the shape of the instrument from which it was taken, the harpsichord, and to our minds is the natural outline of the instrument, its only objection being its largeness.

Although we are indebted to Europe for the invention of Piano Fortes, this country must bear away the palm for the vast and various improvements of the last few years; if our space permitted we would mention some of them, but they fill too long a list to do so without being invidious. But it is undoubtedly a fact, that owing to the superiority of American Manufacture, there are more Pianos made in New York than in any other part of the world, and while thirty years ago, we imported all our instruments, we now scarcely import one, having thus added the monopoly of a most important and lucrative branch of industry to our domestic resources.

Prominent amongst those who have contributed to the improvement of this greatest of instruments, must be ranked the firm of Messrs. RAVEN, BACON & Co., established in 1829.* They have now been over thirty years in business. During this lengthened period they have effected several improvements themselves, and have always encouraged any new invention that promised to be an inprovement; by these means their instruments are now recognised as amongst the best to be had. We recently went over their manufactory, and although it was only a flying visit, thanks to their courteous and lucid explanations, we think we have mastered some of the mysteries of Piano Forte making, which for the benefit of our readers we will detail.

Their factory, situated at 147, 149, 151 Baxter street, extends through to Mulberry street, having a frontage of fifty feet by two hundred feet deep. Part of this area is occupied by the Lumber Yard. In this yard, in lofty piles, are stored the various woods used in the manufacture of Pianos, such as Rosewood, Mahogany, Cherry, Maple, Ash, White Wood, Pine, Ebony, White Holly, Bass Wood, &c. From the Lumber Yard, these woods are taken to the drying rooms situated in the basement, and also on the first floor, where they undergo a thorough drying for three months, being subjected for the whole of that time to a high degree of heat. They are then fit for use, and are taken to the store room, from whence they are taken to the different departments of the five story building as required. Every department has different functions, and although each man may be perfect in his department, no one man could make a perfect Piano. In one room we see the Rim maker, in another the Bottom maker; we pass on through various rooms, and we see the makers of Tops, Legs, Cases, and Keys, the bellyman, the finishers, the fly finishers, the regulators, tuners, varnishers and polishers, the block makers, the lyric action maker, and the stringer. Each of these is a separate branch of business, and it takes from six to nine months before a perfect piano can be turned out of their factory. During their thirty years' experience, they have manufactured about eight thousand pianos, ordinarily employing in the different departments about one hundred men.

Messrs. Raven, Bacon & Co., have their warerooms at 135 Grand street, where they have on hand a beautiful assortment of Pianos, both Grand and Square. They have lately given their especial attention to the Grand, and have succeeded in manufacturing a very superior Piano, which will stand any climate without warping or losing tone. These Pianos are pronounced by judges as being perfect both in tone and make. Let those intending purchasing, pay them a visit.

The following is given as the new mode of parsing, down east, "I court." Court is a verb active, indicative mood, present tense, and agrees with all the girls in the neighborhood.

A lady in an omnibus at Washington espied the great unfinished dome of the capitol, and said innocently, "I suppose those are the gas-works?" "Yes, madam, for the *nation*," was the reply of a fellow-passenger.

An architect proposes to build a "Bachelors' Hall," which will differ from most houses in having no Eves.

GUNPOWDER.

For men (it is reported) dash and vapor
Less on the field of battle than on paper.
Thus in the history of each dire campaign
More carnage loads the newspaper than plain.
                                                DR. WOLCOTT.

Now that "grim-visaged war" has appeared in our midst a few words about this most destructive article may not be out of place. The date of its invention is lost in obscurity; some writers make mention of it as early as A.D. 85; others say it was used by the Arabs at the siege of Mecca, in 690, and others again ascribe the invention of it to Berthold Schwartz, a monk, about the year 1336. But the generally received opinion is, that it was known to the Chinese and Indians, long prior to the Christian era, and was doubtless discovered by accident.

Gunpowder consists of a very intimate mixture of nitre, charcoal, and sulphur. The proportions vary for different kinds, but generally consist of about three-quarters nitre, to one-eighth charcoal, and one-eighth sulphur. The ingredients are separately ground to a fine powder, then mixed, rolled, and again ground, and taken to the corning house to be grained. The mixing process is a very delicate one, as the strength of the powder depends upon the proportions being equally preserved. The powder when grained is passed through a series of sieves, first to separate the dust from it and also the different sized grains; from thence it is taken to the stove and dried, care being taken not to raise the heat so as to dissipate the sulphur.

The theory of the action of gunpowder is this: That particle of it on which a spark falls is immediately heated to a state of ignition, the nitre is decomposed, and its oxygen combines with the charcoal and sulphur which are also heated. The combination extricates as much heat as is sufficient to inflame successively, though rapidly, the remaining mass, liberating carbonic acid, carbonic oxide, and nitrogen, which forms the explosive power of gunpowder.

One of the largest works for the manufacture of this article in this country, or indeed we may say in the world, is that known by the name of the HAZARD POWDER COMPANY. The main works are situated at Hazardville, upon the Scantic river. The Company have also mills at Scitico, East Hartford, Conn., and at Canton in the same state. They have been established for nearly a quarter of a century, and these mills at these various places extend over a distance of more than a mile in length, and half a mile in width; these mills consist in part of eighteen sets of rolling mills, with iron wheels, each wheel weighing eight tons; seven different granulating mills; seven screw presses, and three hydraulic presses of four hundred tons power each, some twenty-five to thirty dusting, sorting, drying, glazing, and packing houses; with extensive saltpetre refineries and magazines; cooper shops, iron and wood machine shops, stables, outhouses, &c. In all over one hundred and twenty-five buildings, giving employment to hundreds of hands, which, notwithstanding the hazardous nature of the business, they find no difficulty in obtaining.

The moving power to set this vast mass of machinery in motion, consists of twenty-five water-wheels and two steam-engines, one being a very large and beautifully constructed low-pressure engine, the whole comprising one of the most complete and perfect gunpowder manufactories in the world.

They manufacture annually over one million dollars' worth of the various brands known as Government, Sporting, Shipping, and Mining Powder, the quality and reputation of which are well known all over this country as well as in Europe. During the Crimean war this Company manufactured ten thousand barrels of powder for the British Government, the English works not being able to turn out sufficient for their consumption, and they had the gratifying information from officers of the British Army, that these ten thousand barrels of powder were of superior quality to any they had used before.

The office of the HAZARD POWDER COMPANY in New York, is at 89 Wall street, corner of Water, and while wishing the house success in their business, which their enterprise deserves, we hope that the article may increase in demand, for although (paradoxical as it may seem) a powerful destroyer, it is yet a benefactor. It levels our roads, bores tunnels for our railroads, clears the channels of our rivers from rocks, helps to dig our canals, and is most useful in our mines. In these it is a powerful agent of civilization, and we hope we may want its utmost aid for many years to come in subduing our vast extent of territory from wilderness to cultivation.

Fanny Fern lately said:—"If one-half of the girls only knew the previous life of the men they marry, the list of old maids would be wonderfully increased."

But the *Boston Post* asks:—"If the men knew, Fanny, what their future lives were to be, wouldn't it increase the list of old maids still further?"

Swinging is said by the doctors to be a good exercise for health, but many a poor wretch has come to his death by it.

REPEATING FIRE-ARMS.

> Then said the mother to her son,
> And pointed to his shield—
> "Come *with it* when the battle's done,
> Or *on it*, from the field."
>
> MONTGOMERY.

We recently paid a visit to the Manufactory of Colt's Patent Fire-arms Manufacturing, Co., at Hartford, Conn., and although we were prepared to find a large establishment, our ideas fell far short of its actual magnitude. At the present moment, the manufactory is running night and day, employing over eleven hundred hands, and so great is the demand for fire-arms of this patent, that even this large force can scarcely supply it. We purpose in the present article giving a description of this manufactory, with some items respecting the origin of this invention, for which we are indebted to a paper read by Col. Colt before the Institution of Civil Engineers in London in 1851.

It appears that, while a very young man, Mr. Colt had paid much attention to the subject of fire-arms. In the paper previously mentioned, he remarks: "The author, living in a country of most extensive frontier, still inhabited by hordes of aborigines, and knowing the insulated position of the enterprising pioneer and his dependence, sometimes alone, on his personal ability to protect himself and family, had often meditated upon the inefficiency of the ordinary double-barrelled gun and pistol, both involving a loss of time in reloading, which was too frequently fatal in the peculiar character of Indian border warfare. By the United States Government, also, it was considered an object of great importance to obtain an effective repeating arm, as the peculiar characteristic of the mode of attack by the mounted Indians was to overwhelm small bodies of American soldiers by rushing down on them in greatly superior numbers, after having drawn their fire, and to dispatch them, while in a comparatively defenceless state, from the necessity of reloading their arms. After much reflection and repeated trials, he effected an arrangement in the construction of revolving fire-arms, without having seen, or being aware, at that period (1829), of any arm more effective than a double-barrelled gun having ever been constructed, and it was only during a visit to Europe, in the year 1835, that he discovered he was not the first person who had conceived the idea of repeating fire-arms with a rotating chambered-breech."

Undoubtedly the whole idea and construction of his wonderfully efficient weapon was entirely original with Colonel Colt, and most likely these are among the prominent reasons of the great triumph of his efforts. Had he been furnished with the results of those who preceded him, probably he would have too nearly followed in their tracks, and thus have been diverted from the goal of success. This hypothesis has, in a measure, been illustrated in some of the minor acts of his life; and we understand that the theory now practised by him is to depend solely on his personal resources. If he wishes to accomplish a certain object, let it be a new application of machinery, or what not, he desires no rehearsal of the efforts of others; but, in his own way, and by his own personal ingenuity, the result is produced.

The original conception of Colonel Colt, in regard to fire-arms, was the combination of a number of long barrels to rotate upon a spindle, by the act of cocking the lock, in the same manner that they have since been made by others, who claim to have originated the plan; but, as objections arose from the weight and bulk of the arm, in his study to obviate them, the idea of a single barrel and a chambered breech suggested itself to him. Although without the pecuniary means of then practically testing his convictions, he made a small wooden model of his conception, which he possesses at the present day. He then assiduously pursued his calling, as a scientific lecturer, and from its rewards procured the aid to manufacture specimen arms, which in their practical results exceeded even his own most sanguine expectations; and in 1835 he received his first patent from the Government of the United States.

After procuring this patent, Colonel Colt's want of pecuniary aid placed him in the situation of most successful inventors, and his only course was to engage the attention of capitalists to form a company, which he succeeded in doing in 1836. This company lasted till 1842, when they had to suspend operations. From that time, till 1847, none were manufactured, and the stock previously in hand was completely exhausted. The Mexican war breaking out in this year, General Taylor, who had witnessed the utility of these weapons in Florida, sent Captain Walker to procure a supply of revolvers from Col. Colt, but not one could be found. Col. Colt, however, was equal to the emergency. He was then looked upon as a ruined man, but he thought otherwise, and at once contracted to furnish the Government one thousand arms. From that day to the present his business has been a constant success, and has resulted in the completion of the most perfect establishment for the manufacture of fire-arms that exists on this or any other continent.

Within the corporate limits of the City of Hartford, immediately below the Little or Mill River, is a section of land, containing about 250 acres, which, owing to its formerly being submerged at the periodical freshets of the Connecticut River, was available at certain seasons only, and then but for grazing. Colonel Colt selected and purchased this spot as his field of operations. His first move was to erect an embankment, or dyke, by which the waters of the Connecticut were entirely and permanently excluded; thus reclaiming the land for building purposes or tillage, as might be desired. This embankment is about two miles long, averaging over one hundred feet wide at the base, and over forty feet in width at the top, and from ten to twenty feet in height. It is built in the most substantial manner, the sides being covered with osier, both for protection and ornament. From the smoothness of the road, and the beautiful scenery in the vicinity, the dyke has become the fashionable drive of the citizens.

The new armory is located about one hundred yards south of the mouth of Little River, immediately inside of the dyke, and fronting on the west side of the Connecticut River. It was finished and operations commenced in it in the Fall of 1855. The ground plan of the principal buildings forms the letter H. It is a massive structure of brown sand-stone, of the variety usually designated " Portland freestone." The front parallel is 500 feet long, 60 wide, and three stories high; at the centre, for about sixty feet of the front, there is a projection of eighteen feet wide, surmounted by a pediment. This forms ample space for hall and stairways to give access to the several stories. On top is the cupola, with a canopy of blue emblazoned with gilt stars, the whole surmounted by a large gilt ball, on which stands a COLT, rampant. The rear parallel is 500 feet long by 40 wide; the centre building is 150 feet long by 60 wide, and three stories high. At each end, between the extremities of the parallels, are two small two-story dwellings, both of which are occupied by the watchman; from these erections to the main buildings are heavy walls, with massive gates; thus the space inclosed by the stone walls is just 500 by 250 feet square. Nearly adjoining on the north, and connected to the main building by a light lattice-work bridge, is a brick building, three stories high, 60 by 75 feet square, and surmounted by a turret and clock. This is occupied by the officers, and as a wareroom.

The motive power is located about the centre of the main building. It consists of a beam engine—cylinder, 36 inches in diameter, 7 feet stroke, fly-wheel 30 feet in diameter, weighing 7 tons. This engine, which is rated at 250 horse-power, is supplied with the well-known "Sickel's Cut-off," which the superintendent and engineer speak of as the most useful and important addition to the steam-engine since the days of Watt. The steam is furnished from two cylindrical boilers, each 22 feet long and 7 feet diameter. The power is carried to the attic by a belt working on the fly-wheel; this belt is 118 feet long by 22 inches wide, and travels at the rate of 2500 feet per minute.

Leaving the office we cross the bridge, pass down through the machine shop, engine room, etc., to the rear parallel, an apartment 40 by 50 feet square, the centre of which is appropriated as the store-room for iron and steel. Large quantities of these materials, in bars and rods, are stored here in charge of a responsible party, whose duty it is to fill the orders from the contractors, and render an accurate statement of such deliveries to the main storekeeper's department. This latter system is universal throughout the establishment—thus the materials of all kinds can be readily accounted for, no matter what their state of transposition.

We now pass into the forge shop, an apartment 40 by 200 feet square, comprising the whole of one arm of the parallel. Along each side range stacks of double-covered forges—the blasts for which, entering and discharging through flues in the walls, carry off the smoke and gases. Here, for the first time in our life, we were in a blacksmith's shop in full operation, yet free from smoke and cinders, and with a pure atmosphere. Several kinds of hammers are used—those most in use, however, being "drops" of a novel construction and peculiar to the establishment; they are raised on the endless screw principle, and tripped by a trigger at the will of the operator. All the parts of the fire-arm composed of iron or steel are forged in swedges, in which, although they may have ever so many preliminary operations, the shape is finally completed at a single blow. That some idea may be formed of the amount of work on a single rifle or pistol, we have determined to state the number of separate operations of each portion, and in each department. We adopt the navy or belt pistol, the weight of which is thirty-eight ounces, as the example. In forging, the number of separate heats are enumerated: lockframe, 2; barrel, 3; lever, 2; rammer, 1; hammer, 2; hand, 2; trigger, 2; bolt, 2; main spring, 2; key, 2; nipples, 2 each, 12; thus we find that no less than *thirty-two* separate and distinct operations, some of which contain in themselves several subdivisions, are required in the forging for a single pistol.

After forging, each piece is inspected, and, if passed, is removed to the annealing ovens, which are situated in the foundry—this latter occupying the opposite arm of the rear parallel, its dimensions also being 40 by 200 feet. The arrangements here for both brass and iron castings are on a liberal scale; the former is mostly for mountings, bullet-moulds, etc.—the latter for machinery. After being annealed, the forgings are immersed in a chemical preparation to cleanse them by removing the scales and dirt; they are now ready for milling, shaping, etc.

It is unnecessary to describe all the operations performed by the machines; a few will render the whole understandable. Taking the lockframe, for instance: they commence by fixing the centre, and drilling and tapping the base for receiving the arbor or breech-pin, which has been previously prepared—the helical grove cut in it, and the lower end screwed—once grasped is firmly fixed into its position, furnishing a definite point from which all the operations are performed, and to which all the parts bear relation. The facing and hollowing of the recoil shield and frame, the cutting and sinking the central recesses, the cutting out all the grooves and orifices, planing the several flat surfaces and shaping the curved parts, prepare the frames for being introduced between hard steel clamps, through which all the holes are drilled, bored and tapped for the various screws; so that, after passing through thirty-three distinct operations, and the little hand-finishing required in removing the burr from the edges, the lock-frame is ready for the inspector. The rotating, chambered cylinder is turned out of cast-steel bars, manufactured expressly for the purpose. The machines, after getting them the desired length, drill centre holes, square up ends, turn for ratchet, turn exterior, smooth and polish, engrave, bore chambers, drill partitions, tap for nipples, cut pins for hammer-rest and ratchet, and screw in nipples. In all there are thirty-six separate operations before the cylinder is ready to follow the lock-frame to the inspector. In the same manner the barrel, forged solidly from a bar of cast steel, is bored and completed to calibre, and is then submitted to the various operations of planing, grooving the lower projection beneath the barrel, with which the base pin is ultimately connected, tapped, and then rifled. The barrel goes through forty-five separate operations on the machines. The other parts are subject to about the following number: lever, 27; rammer, 19; hammer, 28; hand, 20; trigger, 21; bolt, 21; key, 18; sear spring, 12; fourteen screws, seven each, 98; six cones, eight each, 48; guard, 18; handle-strap, 5; stock, 5. Thus it will be observed that the greater part of the labor is completed in this department. Even all the various parts of the lock are made by machinery, each having its relative initial point to work from, and on the correctness of which the perfection depends.

As soon as completed the different parts are carried to the story above, which, with the exception of the machinery and the columns through the centre, is an exact counterpart of the room below. It is designated the Inspecting and Assembling Department. Here the different parts are most minutely inspected; this embraces a series of operations which in the aggregate amount to considerable; the tools to inspect a cylinder, for example, are fifteen in number, each of which must gauge to a hair; the greatest nicety is observed, and it is absolutely impossible to get a slighted piece of work beyond this point. On finishing his examination, the inspector punches his initial letter on the piece inspected, thus pledging his reputation on its quality.

The mountings, consisting of the handle-strap and guard, which are composed of gun-metal, are cast, and afterwards worked up in the machines, in the same manner as the other metal work. The woodwork of the stock is also shaped by machinery.

Each part having been thus far completed in itself, now comes the first uniting, or *assembling*, as the workmen term it. Let us get our navy pistol in shape; to do so we will want a cylinder barrel, lock-frame, hammer, trigger, bolt, key, main-spring, hand, scar-spring, lever, rammer, guard, back-strap, stock, and a number of peculiar screws. These are readily united by the assembler, and our pistol assumes its material shape. It is now numbered; to make it special, we will designate our number as 13,565; the imprint of the establishment, "Address Colonel Sam. Colt, Hartford, Conn.," is also stamped on at this time. It is now carefully taken apart, all the pieces being stamped the particular number of the arm; and thus our barrel, cylinder, etc., each with a quantity of his fellows, are taken away for their final finishing.

Most of the metal work is carried to the dry polishing shop —a room sixty feet square, located in the third story of the centre building. Here it is polished on emery and other wheels, about half a yard in diameter, the operatives sitting at their work, as observed in the illustration. After inspection, the barrels and cylinders are handed over for the blueing process—an operation that requires nicety and practical experience. The ovens for this, as well as for the case-hardening— to which process all the iron work is submitted—as well as the forges for tempering the springs, etc., are located in the forge shop. From the polishers the mountings go to the electroplaters, who occupy a room 25 by 40, in the basement of the office building, where they are plated with silver, and afterwards burnished. The wood work returns to the stock-maker's shop a room 60 by 80, in the third story of the centre building. This is supplied with power saws, planes, morticing, and shaping machines, for wood work, and, as throughout the whole establishment, every means is adopted for labor-saving. The stock then comes back for varnishing and the final finishing.

On their final completion, all the parts are delivered to the general store-keeper's department, a room 60 feet wide by 190 feet long, situated in the second story of the central building, and extending over the rear parallel. All the hand-tools and materials (except the more bulky kinds) are distributed to the workmen from this place; several clerks are required to parcel the goods out, and keep the accounts; in fact, it is a *store*, in the largest sense of the term, and rather on the wholesale principle at that. On the reception of finished, full sets of the parts of the pistols, they are once more carried up to the assembling room; but this time to another corps of artisans. Guided by the numbers, they are once more assembled; and now, although each portion has associated with scores of its fellows, and gone through many distinct operations in distant parts of the establishment, our particular pistol, number 13,565, is re-assembled as first united, and the finished arm is laid on a rack, ready for the prover; of course many others accompany it to the department of this official, which is located in the third story of the rear building. Here each chamber is loaded with the largest charge possible, and practically tested by firing; after which, they are wiped out by the prover, and returned to the inspection department. The inspectors again take them apart, thoroughly clean and oil them, when they are for the last time put together, and placed in a rack for the final inspection. The parts having been so thoroughly examined and tested, it would seem that this last inspection was scarcely necessary; but, after a short observation, we saw several laid aside. Taking up one with a small mark on the barrel—" Why do you reject this?" we inquired. " Pass this to-day, and probably much larger blemishes would appear to-morrow." The order from the Principal is perfection; and a small scratch in the bluing or varnish is sufficient to prevent the arm passing. The finished arm is now returned to the store room; from whence, after being papered, they are sent to the wareroom—situated in the basement of the office building; from this they are sent to nearly every portion of the habitable globe.

We have thus given a brief review of Colt's arms manufacturing company, which our want of space has forced us to condense so much, that we fear we have failed to convey a very forcible idea of its extent; a volume could be written on the subject, and even then leave room for more, so numerous and varied are the different operations carried on in this establishment.

This company has an office, and samples of their manufactures, at No. 240 Broadway, New York.

Why will America's emblem outlive those of England, France, Ireland, and Scotland? Because the rose must fade—the lily droop—the shamrock die—the thistle wither, but the stars are eternal.

John Reeve was accosted by an elderly man with a small bottle of gin in his hand, " Pray, sir, I beg your pardon, is this the way to the workhouse?" John, pointing to the bottle, gravely said, " No, my man, but that is!"

SHOT, LEAD, PIPE, &c.

Ah me! what perils do environ
The man that meddles with cold iron.
                                                BUTLER.

Unquestionably the most extensive establishment for the manufacture of the above-named articles is that of Messrs. THOMAS OTIS LEROY & Co., Nos. 261 and 263 Water street, New York.

The facilities of this firm for the manufacture of lead pipe, sheet lead, pure block tin pipe, sheet tin, drop and buck shot, bar lead, musket and rifle balls, are unsurpassed, having a large and well regulated factory, and machinery of the most improved construction for the business. Their machinery for the manufacture of lead and tin pipe, is superior to any other in use, from the perfection of the article it produces; and the privilege of using it, is enjoyed by this firm exclusively. Their drop shot is also manufactured under a patent, which, by a very simple operation, furnishes a quality of shot which has never been excelled. The quality of their buck shot and balls is superior to any other made in this country, as it is compressed and much more perfect than possible to make it in any other way. They are the only manufacturers who make buck shot and bullets by this method.

This establishment consumes annually about 6,000 tons of pig lead, besides large quantities of block tin.

They keep a large stock constantly on hand of U. S. Minie musket and rifle balls, and every description of round and conical bullets on hand or made to order.

Hood once admonished a gossiping Christian to beware lest her piety should prove, after all, to be nothing better than mag-piety.

FANCY GOODS, FOREIGN AND DOMESTIC.

> We live in deeds, not years—in thoughts, not breaths—
> In feelings, not in figures on a dial;—
> We should count time by heart-throbs. He most lives,
> Who thinks most—feels the noblest—acts the best.
>   BUTLER.

The list of goods under this heading has of late years been so continually increased, that at the present moment it would require a book of considerable magnitude to convey anything like an accurate idea of the almost endless variety of goods that are required for a stock of any of the first class dealers of New York. As our space does not admit of a detailed account of them we shall content ourselves with a brief description of one of the largest fancy goods stores in the city, together with some facts and figures which may prove of interest, and at the same time serve to convey some idea of the importance of this trade.

We allude to the firm of *Cary, Howard, Sanger & Co.*, who have been in the business nearly thirty-five years, during which lengthened period they have had the opportunity of contributing materially to the development of the manufacture of Domestic Fancy Goods. In the earlier stages of their business a very large number of articles were obtained exclusively from abroad. Now, these same articles are mostly manufactured here. Messrs. C. H. S. & Co. early perceived the advantage to the country of manufacturing at home, instead of importing, and assisted both pecuniarily and otherwise, several manufacturers, to establish themselves, and the consequences have been so much more labor employed, and so many more of the resources of our country developed. For their *own* contribution to home labor, they established a manufactory for *Horn* Combs, at Newark, N. J., and for *Ivory* Combs, at Deep River, Conn., both of which are of the largest class, and in point of equipments and *quality* of productions, second to none.

To give our readers an idea of their extensive establishment, let them imagine a six-story iron building of very beautiful architecture, having a frontage on two of the principal business streets of New York of 50 feet, extending through 150 feet, and on opening any of the doors on the first floor see the whole of this extensive area at one glance, there being nothing to obstruct the view save the iron columns supporting the floors above; between these columns are innumerable counters with passages running at right angles. On these counters, to the right, to the left, and in front, are displayed the goods the product of the taste and ingenuity of three continents, yes, perhaps we might say four continents, although Africa does not at the present moment contribute much to the tasteful ingenuity of the world. The eye cannot take in at one glance the immense variety of goods presented to it. Prominently we see the larger and more valuable articles of Bronzes, Jewelry, Watches, Clocks, Dressing Cases; but on closer inspection we find the more indispensable and unpretending articles of domestic use. Here are Combs, Buttons, Sewing Silk, Stationery, &c. This floor forms a kind of sample-room from which to select the smaller kinds of fancy goods, and the more valuable articles of jewelry, &c., while the great bulk of the stock is stored in the floors below. Descending to the basement we see a very large assortment of Perfumery, Threads, Spool Cottons, Brushes, Suspenders, Tapes, Hooks and Eyes, Pins, and other bulky articles; here also is the office of the entry and shipping clerks, which is a scene of incessant activity in the busy seasons.

In the floor below this is the packing and store-room for whole packages, which are transferred from the street to this floor, and *vice versa*, by means of hoistways of very ingenious machinery. These floors are forty feet longer than the others, and capable of containing an immense number of packages, which are stored with such perfect order and system, that any special one can be reached at any moment.

From the street-floor we ascend by a large double staircase to another, in which is arranged the Fancy Hardware, Cutlery, Guns, Pistols, Needles, Musical Instruments, &c., which can only be properly and advantageously exhibited in light and dry rooms.

We have thus briefly enumerated some of the principal articles exhibited in the store occupied by Messrs. C. H. S. & Co.; to go into detail would be impossible, as they have over *fifteen hundred different kinds of merchandize*, each of these being again subdivided into *ten times the number of varieties*, and perhaps even more than that.

The Store at Nos. 105 and 107 Chambers, and 89 and 91 Reade street, was built in 1857, by Mr. W. H. Cary, the senior member of the firm, at a cost of $200,000. Being designed for their business, it may be regarded as the most complete, spacious, and elegant warehouse of any in this trade in the world, while the beautiful architecture of the two fronts, both of the same design, forms quite an attractive feature of our city. In this store they employ over fifty persons, while their factories at Newark and Deep River, for the making of raw-horn and ivory combs of every description, give employment to hundreds of mechanics and laborers.

It may well be imagined that a business of so varied and intricate a character would require the exercise of much forethought and good management. With a large class of buyers scattered broadcast throughout this and other countries, a peculiar system becomes necessary, and it is pleasing to observe throughout the establishment the constant exercise of that wisdom, vigilance, and harmonious arrangement, which always bespeak the qualifications of the true business man.

One of the peculiar advantages of a business such as we have described, where, as before stated, are to be found upwards of fifteen hundred different articles, is, that it saves to purchasers much time and perplexity, ordinarily occasioned by seeking goods at various places.

Having thus briefly given an outline sketch of the largest and most complete establishment of the kind in the world, we conclude by saying that this house alone is the most satisfactory evidence of the triumphs of American excellence in commerce and the fine arts.

The single lady of a certain age is a personage scarcely at all seen, at any rate in her proper position, except in England. In Roman Catholic countries she takes refuge in a convent; she is hardly considered respectable; whereas here, she is respectability itself! The old maid of old novels and plays, indeed, prim, censorious, and spiteful, is disappearing. In her place we have a most cheerful, contented, benevolent, and popular lady, seldom behind the fashion or behind the news and literature of the day—beloved by nephews and nieces, married brothers and sisters, and cousins; a tower of strength in times of sickness and family troubles; a favorite visitor, yet not always visiting, nor staying too long; sometimes, on the contrary, having a snug little home of her own, where pet nieces and nephews spend a few days most delightfully; a guardian angel to the poor; a valuable auxiliary to the clergyman and clergyman's wife; in high esteem and respect among the tradespeople; a famous letter-writer, and the fabricator of most beautiful fancy work. Of this genus we are privileged to know several specimens, some of whom, we are bold to hope, will bridle when they read this little account, and say, with a pleased, half-doubtful look: "Well, I'm sure, this can't be me!" Yes, it is you, aunt Kate and aunt Maria, and ever so many aunts with pretty names, and who have been pretty young women in your time, and who now have something dearer than beauty. You are the salt of the country; as long as you are the objects and subjects of such warm and kindly feeling, you greatly contribute to the support of the social affections.

NEW YORK HOSPITAL,

Situated between Duane and Worth streets, is a most important benevolent institution, of which, indeed, there is a goodly number in New York. It dates back to 1771, when it was founded by the Earl of Dunmore, who was at that time governor of the colony. The accommodation for patients, which of late years has been greatly enlarged, is very extensive, and excellent in every respect. It is a receptacle in cases of sudden accidents. It is not altogether gratuitous; but, to such as are able to pay a little, it offers most important advantages—four dollars a week commanding the best medical attendance, besides nursing and medicine. The students, too, have the benefit, for a small annual fee, of accompanying the surgeons in their rounds.

A new theatre is now nearly completed on Broadway above 13th st., having an entrance on the latter and running through to Fourth Avenue. We should have liked to have given some particulars about it, but when we applied for information, sending in to his H. J. H., the lessee, our piece of pasteboard, that magnate declined seeing us or giving any particulars, so we can only satisfy the public there is a building said to be intended for a theatre located on that spot; and we will further inform them, that should they at any time visit it they will find exactly opposite the 13th street entrance a most genial clever fellow by the name of Thorp, whose oysters and other refreshments have been celebrated from time immemorial; should they experience a vacuum in the interior (which nature abhors) he will satisfy it with the choicest the market affords. The principal entrance to the hotel is 838 Broadway.

ENGRAVING.

Such is the strength of art, rough things to shape,
And of rude commons, rich enclosures make.
HOWELL.

GEORGE WASHINGTON.
Engraved on Wood and Electrotyped by A. H. Jocelyn, 60 Fulton st., New York.

ALBERT H. JOCELYN, 60 Fulton street.

We have abundant evidence to prove that the art of Engraving is of the remotest antiquity. In the early history of the Jews, frequent mention is made of it in the Bible. Thus, from the Book of Exodus we have the command given to Moses, "to make a plate of pure gold and grave upon it, like the engraving of a signet, holiness to the Lord." And again, "to take two Onyx stones and grave on them the names of the children of Israel, according to their birth, with the work of an engraver on stone." Both these passages distinctly imply the practice of gem and seal engraving, and also of engraving on metal plates, a knowledge of which, among other arts, was doubtless acquired by the Israelites from the Egyptians during their bondage.

From Herodotus, we learn that one of the earliest uses to which engraving was applied among the Greeks was, the delineation of maps on metal plates. He says (v. 49), that "Aristagoras appeared before the King of Sparta with a tablet of brass in his hand, on which was inscribed every part of the habitable world, the seas, and the rivers; and to this he pointed as he spoke of the several countries between the Ionian sea and Susa." The date of this event was 500 B.C.

That an art so abundantly capable of diffusing all kinds of knowledge, should have been extensively practised from the most remote antiquity, without its applicability to printing being discovered, is a curious subject for reflection; and we can only imagine that its not having led to this discovery, was for the want of material to print on; as when the manufacture of paper from linen rags was discovered at the latter end of the fourteenth century, the invention of printing very shortly followed it.

The earliest wood engraving, with a date attached to it, that we have any knowledge of, is that known as the St. Christopher, which is dated 1423; but no impression from an engraved *printed plate* has been found anterior to 1461. Germany and Italy both claim the invention, but Italy, we think, has the best title to it, and it is now generally conceded to that country.

The art of Wood Engraving has made most rapid progress during the last few years in this country, and no one individual has contributed more to that progress than Mr. A. H. JOCELYN, the proprietor of the "New York Wood Engraving Establishment," of No. 58 and 60 Fulton street. In this establishment, none but the most competent artists are engaged, and he is, therefore, enabled to produce work which, in beauty and accuracy of design, fineness of finish, and boldness of execution, cannot be surpassed. Mr. J. gives his personal attention to the fulfilment of special orders, and he has constantly on hand several hundred original illustrations, suitable for all purposes, and is engraving, from time to time, numerous designs for the artistic printer; to such and all requiring wood engravings, we can recommend Mr. Jocelyn, as they will find in his establishment the art carried to perfection in all its beautiful and interesting details.

Adversity overcome is the brightest glory, and willingly undergone, the greatest virtue. Sufferings are but the trials of gallant spirits.

A lively Hibernian exclaimed, at a party where Theodore Hook shone as the evening star, "Och, Master Theodore, but you're the *hook* that nobody can *bate*."

BABBITT'S PREMIUM PORTABLE FENCE.

> Beside yon straggling fence, that skirts the way
> With blossom'd furze, unprofitably gay,
> There, in his noisy mansion, skill'd to rule
> The village master taught his little school.
>
> GOLDSMITH.

Farmers and agriculturists have long experienced the want of a good strong endurable portable fence. Fencing in has hitherto been the heaviest unproductive outlay in the farm, and consequently a great national tax; any improvement therefore that will save time, facilitate operations, and diminish expenditure, must be equally a national benefit, and we think the inventor of this fence has succeeded in effecting it.

At present many varieties of fence are in use, both of iron and wood, of almost all conceivable shapes and forms, from the rough worm fence of the backwoodsman to the highly ornamental fence of the gentleman farmer, the first costing an immense amount of labor to create, and the latter a large expenditure; both useful in their way, but neither adapted to all the wants of a large farm, especially a cattle farm, where it is oftentimes very desirable to be able to part off at certain seasons parts of fields for pasturage and other parts for cultivation. In such case the observing farmer will readily perceive the advantage of a PORTABLE FENCE, that can be easily removed from place to place as occasion may require, at a very small cost of time and labor, and one that can be equally as well used permanently as temporarily. The annexed engraving will illustrate the construction of this fence. It will be observed that the six cross rails cut square are inserted diagonally in upright pillars resting on the ground; these uprights are in two parts braced together by an iron band on the upper end, while the corner pillars have four equal separate sides tapering

upwards, held together in the same manner. It will thus easily be perceived how strong a fence it will form when up, and how easily it can be taken apart and moved from place to place. Among the advantages of this fence are the following:

1. It is very simple—can be put up and taken apart with great ease and rapidity.

2. The rails are square, put up diagonally, thereby shedding rain, no part touching the ground, consequently it is the most durable fence made.

3. It is heavier at the bottom than at the top; winds take but a slight hold of it.

4. When taken apart it occupies the least possible space, and is very conveniently transported.

5. Unlike most other fences, it beautifies the appearance of fields. It cannot become a covert for foul seeds and weeds.

6. Harmonizing with enlightened agriculture, by avoiding unnecessary or useless outlay, it enables the farmer to dispense with all interior fencing, except portions of his pasture grounds for stock grazing. When one portion is eaten off, the fence is removed, enclosing another portion; and thus the stock have the benefit of fresh pastures.

7. It is convenient for fencing off portions of large fields, parks, and lawns—for railroads and other public works.

8. The price of Farm Fence of six rails of good material is from ten to twelve cents per running foot.

9. Forty rods of it can be taken up and put down in a day by one man.

It is made of oak, hemlock, or pine, and can be made ornamental by attaching caps to the posts.

The inventor has many testimonials from persons in this State and New Jersey, who have this fence in use, showing its efficiency under all circumstances; and some who have it in most exposed situations further assert that the wind has no effect upon it, neither is it liable to derangement by frost; but, on the contrary, in the winter it is of great use in preventing the snow from drifting. These considerations, combined with the advantages of *economy, portability, and strength*, will, we think, prove it an invaluable article to every farmer and planter.

Should any person interested desire to see or learn farther about this fence, the Company will gladly furnish them every information at the office of

THE NEW YORK FENCE COMPANY,

No. 112 William Street, New York,

W. SHATTUCK, Agent.

To whom all orders should be addressed.

As my wife, at the window, one day
  Stood watching a man with a monkey,
A cart came by with a "broth of a boy,"
  Who was driving a stout little donkey.
To my wife then I spoke, by way of a joke,
  "There's a relation of yours in that carriage."
To which she replied, as the donkey she spied,
  "Ah, yes, a relation—by marriage!"

FIRE-PROOF SAFES.

Wise men ne'er sit and wail their loss,
But cheerly seek how to redress their harm.
                                    SHAKSPEARE.

The discovery and invention of Fire-Proof Safes was a triumph of no inconsiderable magnitude, and the invaluable advantages which their possession has secured the business man are too well known to require encomium. For a period of nearly twenty years Mr. SILAS C. HERRING has stood at the head of his business, and his productions, which bear the name of "Champion," have received unqualified approbation of the leading business men of the country. The resources of Messrs. HERRING & Co. are unlimited, as may be inferred from the fact that they employ in their manufacturing department a force of nearly 300 hands. At their establishment, on the corner of Murray street and Broadway, and in the hands of their agents, they have usually a stock of from 900 to 1200 safes, while their annual sales do not fall short of between $300,000 and $400,000. The principle of Herring's Patent Champion Safe, and the process of manufacture, are thus briefly explained:

"The metal portion of these Safes consists of the stoutest and toughest wrought bar and plate iron, and the space between the outer and inner surfaces is filled with a chemical preparation which is the most perfect non-conductor of heat yet discovered, and which cannot be affected or penetrated by fire. This fact has been established beyond question by the results of many experiments, attested by persons of the highest respectability. In every trial to which the *genuine* Herring Safe has been subjected, whether accidental, in burning buildings, or by agreement, for the purpose of competition, its fire-proof properties have proved immeasurably superior to those of any (so called) fire-proof safe ever manufactured. By an improvement upon the original Salamander, introduced by the present owner of the patent right, the interior is rendered wholly impervious to damp, and books, papers, and jewelry might be preserved in one of his safes for a century without contracting a blemish from mould or mildew. To guard against counterfeits, every safe from the manufactory of the proprietor, and sold by him and his agents, has a brass plate in front bearing his name."

So great is the confidence which the proprietors repose in the efficiency of their renowned safes, that they boldly offer the handsome sum of $1000 to any person that can show that a Herring's Patent Champion Safe ever failed to preserve its contents in an accidental fire.

The Messrs. HERRING & Co. are well known to the whole community as enterprising and most reliable business men, being free and liberal in all their business transactions, and fully up to the times in all that constitutes the ingredients of success. The style of the firm is thus designated:

S. C. HERRING & CO.,

PATENTEES AND MANUFACTURERS OF

HERRING'S PATENT CHAMPION FIRE AND BURGLAR PROOF SAFES, WITH HALL'S PATENT POWDER-PROOF LOCK.

SOLE MANUFACTURERS OF

CRYGIER'S PATENT CHANGEABLE POWDER-PROOF LOCK, WITHOUT KEY OR KEYHOLE.

ALSO, SOLE PROPRIETORS OF

JONES' PATENT PERMUTATION BANK LOCK.

The above Safes and Locks both received separate Medals at the World's Fair, London, in 1851, and Crystal Palace, New York, 1853-4.

WAREHOUSE, NO. 251 BROADWAY, CORNER OF MURRAY STREET,

(OPPOSITE CITY HALL),

NEW YORK.

THE BANKING SYSTEM.

Gold is the strength, the sinews of the world;
The health, the soul, the beauty most divine;
A mask of gold hides all deformities;
Gold is heaven's physic—life's restorative.
          DECKER.

The Banking System, as identified with the foreign and domestic trade of the Union, necessarily commands an important position in this work. Agriculture, manufactures, and commerce share equally in the benefits of circulation and currency, from the fact that the United States has no national institution, like those of Europe, to create a general system of banking. New York, being acknowledged at the head of the foreign and domestic exchanges of the Union, requires and has adopted a system of her own; hence the reason for the adjustment of the balances here, and the establishment of a clearing house.

Without entering into details respecting the merits of the general banking system throughout the country, we may here casually remark, that of late years private banking institutions, as affecting the convenience of business men, have found great favor with the public; they have rapidly increased in number, and are now to be found in successful operation in various parts of the country. Prominent among them is the well known banking house of DUNCAN, SHERMAN & Co. The building occupied by this firm is a fine brown-stone structure, situated on the corner of Pine and Nassau-streets. The house was originally established in 1851, by Messrs. Alexander Duncan, Watts Sherman, and W. Ruther Duncan, and has since added to the firm the names of Charles II. Dobney and David Duncan; all of whom have been practically educated to their business, and whose enlarged experience has imparted a reputation to their house second to none in the country. The business transacted by this establishment relates to general banking business. They receive deposits, and make loans and discounts, the same as the city banks, grant letters for the Indies, China, Europe, etc.; also issue circular letters and circular notes for travellers, available in all parts of the globe, embracing the greatest convenience and security. With regard to interest, they allow such sums on current balances as the activity and value of the account will justify. The entire business of the firm, in fact, is conducted upon a sure, solid, and systematic basis, and as affecting the convenience and accommodation of the public, may be regarded as a highly useful institution. Private banking concerns conducted upon the principle adopted by this house should ever receive the sanction and approbation of the public.

Promises.—More persons have suffered and been ruined by making promises, and by believing in those who made them, than by any misfortune or calamity within the circle of human life.

New pumping machines are now being erected at New Orleans; they are guaranteed to throw 12,500,000 gallons of water, for city use, 150 feet high every twenty-four hours.

"Taking them one with another," said Sydney Smith, "I believe my congregation to be the most exemplary observers of the religious ordinances; for the poor keep all the fasts and the rich keep all the feasts."

PHOTOGRAPHY UPON PORCELAIN WARES.

> Art is wondrous long;
> Yet to the wise her paths are ever fair,
> And patience smiles, though genius may despair.
> HOLMES.

On the 30th August, 1859, there issued from the Patent Office of these United States one of the most novel and elegant inventions in the art-world yet patented in the present century. We allude to the art of photographing on porcelain, the product of American genius and perseverance, which has successfully accomplished what Europeans have vainly been endeavoring to effect for years past. This is no small triumph when we come to consider that the celebrated English manufacturer of porcelain and china ware, Mr. Wedgewood, and the equally well known Fox Talbot, have spent months of toil and industrious research to effect the desired object, and that, too, backed with all the means and appliances that wealth could furnish, together with their well known ingenuity and perseverance, and yet have signally failed in its accomplishment.

Highly beautiful as photographs are in their present condition, this invention (the successful effort of Professor PEIN, of New Jersey) has added double lustre to them. The photograph on paper ordinarily presents a dull and sombre appearance; the features and the likeness of course are there, but the vivid life appearance is wanting. This in this new invention is reversed. There, on the contrary, the object presented to the eye stands out in bold relief, not looking, as it is, a picture on a flat surface, but appearing as a projecting substance, heightened in distinctness by the delicacy and vividness by which every mark is developed on the polished surface of the porcelain. There are other advantages also connected with this invention. They can be as well transferred to irregular and uneven as to flat surfaces. Thus, instead of having our tables and mantels loaded with porcelain ornaments covered with unmeaning landscapes, or even artistic, tasty groups of flowers, we can by this process have them covered with portraits of dear loved friends, perhaps far away, or some well remembered landscape, or perhaps some wild mountain scene, or other scenes endeared by old associations upon which memory loves to linger.

Imagine for an instant the face of beauty instantaneously and indelibly transferred to a mantel vase, or to a humbler breakfast cup, or to any other china article that can be possibly manufactured; and that too with an unimpeachable accuracy of outline and a minuteness of shadow rivalling if not excelling the most elaborate products of manual labor, excelling the best productions in accuracy and reliability of features, and you will confess these Porcelain Photographs a marvel of ingenuity, even in this ingenious age. We had supposed the art of photography had been applied to nearly all the uses to which it was capable, but we found Shakspeare was right in saying "There are more things in heaven and earth than are dreamed of in man's philosophy."

Some may think these are luxuries. Doubtless they are, as are all things merely ornamental. But they are inexpensive luxuries, the cost of them little exceeding the ordinary cost of the ornament, and far exceeding them in value as mementoes of the loved or of the past.

We fear we have failed to delineate in our brief article half the beauties of this splendid invention, but we advise such as can to visit the rooms of the AMERICAN PORCELAIN PHOTOGRAPH COMPANY, located at 781 Broadway, and see for themselves. We are sure they can spend a very pleasant hour there. Those who reside in the country, and are desirous of transferring to some porcelain ornament the likeness of themselves or friends, or any vignette or landscape, can have it done by forwarding an accurate photograph on paper, which can be transferred to the vase or article desired.

Any desired information will be gladly given on addressing
THE AMERICAN PORCELAIN PHOTOGRAPH COMPANY,
781 Broadway, New York.

Peppermint, as an article of commerce, is largely grown in Lake county, Ohio. This year over $4000 have been paid to the producers of this article, and in Painsville the oil is worth $12.50 per gallon.

The Savings Banks in Rhode Island have deposits to the amount of $9,163,760 in the names of 35,405 persons. Three of the banks are in Providence, and these have $4,344,061, and 17,709 depositors.

Tuscany is so rich in metallic ores that ships in the channel of Piombino have to allow for the variation of the needle. Sardinia has begun to utilize these mineral riches.

A Western editor thinks sewing girls cannot be expected to compete with sewing-machines, for they haven't such iron constitutions.

The amount of lead shipped from the Galena mines last year was 18,553,211 pounds, valued at $1,028,442.10.

MILITARY BOOKS.

> 'Tis in books the chief
> Of all things to be plain and brief.
> BUTLER.

D. VAN NOSTRAND,

BOOKSELLER, PUBLISHER, AND IMPORTER.

Aristotle tells us that the alphabet was invented to record sound. "Letters," he remarks, "are marks of words, and as words are sounds, significant letters are marks of such sounds." This we know to be correct, and can imagine to be the idea of the inventors of the system, the credit of which, we think, is deservedly accorded to the Phœnicians. Writing was an art of exceedingly slow growth; at first it was pictorial, then as the records became voluminous the scribes were obliged to abridge the representations, and thus gradually and by very slow degrees, the pictures were superseded by the signs of sounds, or in other words, letters were invented. But even after the invention of this invaluable and imperishable art, writing made but slow progress. This, as we mentioned in a previous article, was doubtless owing greatly to the want of material to write upon; paper was not known, and we read that the earliest articles used for this purpose, were plates of lead, copper, the bark of trees, stone, bricks, wood, ivory, and leaves of the palm-tree. Later leather was used, and speedily after the introduction of this, parchment, made from the skins of goats and sheep, was produced, and has been one of the great means of handing down to us the records of past ages. The first books were in the form of blocks or tablets, the square form so much in use now was known to the ancients, but not much valued; when the leather and parchment came into use it was found convenient to make the books into rolls, and the volume when extended would be probably two or three feet in width, by 50 or 100 feet in length; we expect few of our readers would care to peruse such a volume now. As a little item of interest to many, we would mention that the word volume is a word of very ancient origin, derived from the fact of the leaves from the palm, the inner bark of the lime, ash, maple, and elm, being used for writing on; which, when rolled up together, were called *volumen*, a mass, now, *anglicè, volume*. Notwithstanding the immense labor required to produce a volume in those early days, we are told that the library of Alexandria furnished sufficient fuel to the 4,000 baths of that city for *six months*, when the library was destroyed by the order of Caliph Omar, A.D. 642. What a world of mind and thought was there lost never to be regained.

We have given above a few hasty facts about the origin of letters as introductory to speaking of the works of the publisher whose name heads this article. Mr. Van Nostrand has been in the business from his earliest youth, and has recently devoted his special attention to the publishing of military and scientific works; in fact, for naval and military books his house is, "par excellence," the great depôt of the United States, as will be seen by the following catalogue of some of the books he publishes.

Lt. Col. BURNS' NAVAL AND MILITARY TECHNICAL DICTIONARY of the French Language. In two parts, French-English, 1 vol. Crown 8vo. $2 50.

THE SIEGE OF BOMARSUND, 1854. Translated from the French by an Army Officer. 12mo. 75 cts.

RIFLES AND RIFLE PRACTICE.—An Elementary Treatise upon the Theory of Rifle Firing. By Captain C. M. Wilcox, U.S.A. 1 vol. 12mo. With Illustrations. $1 75.

THE ARTILLERIST'S MANUAL. Illustrated by Engravings. By Capt. John Gibbon, U.S.A. 8vo. $5.

AUSTRIAN INFANTRY TACTICS. Translated by Capt. C. M. Wilcox, Seventh Regiment, U.S. Infantry. 1 vol. 12mo. Cloth. $1.

EVOLUTIONS OF FIELD BATTERIES OF ARTILLERY. Translated from the French. By Gen. Robert Anderson, U.S.A. 32mo. Cloth, 33 plates. $1.

THE HAND-BOOK OF ARTILLERY for the Service of the United States. By Capt. Joseph Roberts, U.S.A. 18mo. 75 cts.

A COURSE OF INSTRUCTION in Ordnance Gunnery. By Capt. J. G. Benton, Ordnance Department, U.S.A. 1 vol. 8vo. $5.

NEW MANUAL OF THE BAYONET. By Capt. I. C. Kelton, U.S.A. $1.75.

DICTIONARY of all Officers in the Army of the United States, from 1789 to January 1st, 1860, and of the Navy and Marine Corps. By Col. Chas. K. Gardner. 2d edit. with Supplement. 1 vol. $3.

SCHOOL OF THE GUIDES. By Col. Eugene Le Gal, 55th Regiment N.Y.S.M. 18mo. 50 cts.

THE HAND-BOOK FOR ACTIVE SERVICE, invaluable to both Privates and Officers. By Capt. Egbert L. Vielé, late U.S.A., Capt. of Engineers 7th Regt., National Guard, N.Y. 12mo. $1.

NOTES ON SEA-COAST DEFENCE. By Major J. G. Barnard, U.S. Corps of Engineers. 8vo. $1 50.

THE DANGERS AND DEFENCES OF NEW YORK. By Major J. G. Barnard, Corps of Engineers, U.S. Army. 25 cts.

A TABULAR STATEMENT of the Composition of the French Army on a War Footing. By Capt. C. M. Wilcox, U.S. Army. 25 cts.

A TABULAR STATEMENT of the Composition of the Austrian Army on a War Footing. By Capt. C. M. Wilcox, U.S. Army. 25 cts.

CAPTAIN J. H. WARD, U.S. NAVY. Naval Ordnance and Gunnery. $2.

KELTON'S NEW MANUAL OF THE SWORD EXERCISE. Plates. $1 75.

BERRIMAN'S SWORD PLAY without a Master. $1.

CAPTAIN GRAFTON'S (U.S.A.) CAMP AND MARCH. 75 cts.

JOMINI'S CAMPAIGN OF WATERLOO. 75 cts.

A MILITARY DICTIONARY. Comprising Information on raising and keeping Troops, Actual Service, &c. By Lt.-Col. Henry L. Scott, U.S.A. One large volume, 8vo. half mor. $5.

This latter book, the Military Dictionary, by Col. Scott (son-in-law of the veteran Gen. Scott), is a work that must prove invaluable to officers; the information it contains entitles it more to the character of a Cyclopedia than to that of a Dictionary. Besides giving the full technology of the Military Art, it supplies the latest facts connected with the improvements of Cannon, Fire Arms, &c. It should be in the hands of every one of our volunteer officers.

These books, as we said before, are only a very small part of his catalogue; but those interested in military and naval matters will find every work they may need at his establishment. All the best foreign works on military and naval subjects are imported by him as soon as they issue from the press. He also makes a specialty of scientific works, and has the most complete stock of both American and Foreign always on hand; and from his long experience in the book business, he can supply either public or private libraries on the most liberal terms. Paris, London, Leipsig, Dresden, &c., the great centres of European Literature, contribute by almost every steamer to swell his stock, and we can only recommend all in search of the class of books we have named to visit him, as they will be sure to find them. His address is D. Van Nostrand, 192 Broadway, cor. John street.

"What are wages here?" asked a laborer of a boy. "I don't know, sir." "What does your father get on Saturday night?" "Get?" said the boy, "why, he gets as tight as a brick."

"I go through my work," as the needle said to the idle boy. "But not till you are hard pushed," as the idle boy said to the needle.

www.ingramcontent.com/pod-product-compliance
Lightning Source LLC
Chambersburg PA
CBHW020241170426
43202CB00008B/172